RACE & CLASS

A JOURNAL FOR BLACK AND THIRD WORLD LIBERATION

Volume 36   July-September 1994   Number 1

© Institute of Race Relations 1994
ISSN 0306 3968

Cover Design by Mick Keates
Cover photo by Steve Smith/Andes Press Agency
Typeset by Nancy White
Printed by the Russell Press, Nottingham

MATTHEW CARR

El Salvador: two cheers for democracy?*

The war ... is now entering its final phase. We do not believe that the establishment of a Popular Revolutionary Government is very far off in the future. And if the United States does intervene directly, El Salvador will be the tomb of the US marines.

Salvador Carpio, FMLN Commander (1980)[1]

The most important and innovative premise of the Salvadoran revolution is that no one won total victory. A war that had no military victor has established a new equilibrium and rules of the game for political and economic competition and transformed civil society into the winner.

Joachín Villalobos, FMLN Commander (1993)[2]

In front of the National Palace in San Salvador's Plaza Barrios, an evangelical preacher is haranguing a small group of onlookers from beneath an umbrella. A few yards away, next to the unobtrusive monument erected by the FMLN to commemorate the triumph of democracy in El Salvador, a group of wasted-looking school kids are sharing a bag of glue, oblivious to the two policemen carrying automatic rifles standing just behind them. Traditionally the focal point for demonstrations and political gatherings in the capital, the Plaza Barrios has become a microcosm of the crime and misery in the downtown area, and its grey, dingy appearance bears little trace of the

Matthew Carr is a writer and freelance journalist, living in Spain, who was in El Salvador in 1993.
* See also in this issue Matthew Carr's Commentary piece, 'El Salvador: birth of a new culture'.

Race & Class, 36, 1 (1994)

currents of Salvadoran history that have passed through the square. It was here, on 20 May 1979, on the steps of the still-derelict Metropolitan Cathedral, later devastated by the 1986 earthquake, that twenty-five unarmed demonstrators were killed and seventy wounded before the cameras of foreign journalists, in a televised massacre that brought the savagery of El Salvador's rulers to the world's attention for the first time. In this same square also, on 1 February 1992, 30,000 people gathered to celebrate the historic first public appearance of the five FMLN commanders since the end of the civil war.

These two dates encapsulate the most terrible period in Salvadoran history, from the initial repression of the popular movement in the late 1970s to the ferocious civil war in which more than 100,000 people were killed or disappeared, tens of thousands maimed or disabled and more than one million people became refugees or went into exile. No statistics can convey the full impact of the last great battle of the Cold War on this small central American republic. Even by civil war standards, the Salvadoran war was an exceptionally cruel and destructive conflict, which left few people in the country unaffected. Subsidised by billions of dollars in military and economic aid from the world's most powerful industrial nation, with training and logistical support supplied by the counter-insurgency specialists in the Pentagon, the Salvadoran armed forces launched total war against the FMLN and its civilian bases of support. That the FMLN not only survived this onslaught, but eventually forced their enemies to the negotiating table, is a tribute to the organisation's political and military skills and, above all, to the enormous heroism and self-sacrifice of the men, women and even children who fought and supported the Frente throughout the years of conflict.

At the same time, the support that the FMLN received in some areas was never enough for it to win the war. The intervention of the United States was decisive in preventing the disintegration of the Salvadoran armed forces, while the FMLN was unable to spark the nationwide popular insurrection in El Salvador which had brought the Sandinistas to power in Nicaragua. The result was a long war of attrition, in which both sides controlled large swathes of territory without either of them being able to inflict a decisive defeat on the other. It was this protracted military stalemate, combined with the changed international situation at the end of the 1980s, which finally obliged both sides to seek a negotiated solution to the conflict.

The signing of the Chapultepec Peace Accords in January 1992, following three years of complex and difficult negotiations, marked the end of the war and the beginning of a new era in Salvadoran history. In addition to ending the war, the Accords contained a wide-ranging series of agreements designed to ensure the demilitarisation of El Salvador and establish the political foundations for a new civil society.

In return for a drastic reduction in the size of the armed forces, the dismantling of the allied repressive organisations allied to the military and the establishment of a Truth Commission to investigate human rights abuses committed during the war, the FMLN agreed to demobilise its forces and compete in the electoral process as a political party. In addition, a series of representative institutions were established to oversee the reconstruction of the country and address some of the most severe socio-economic problems, and arrangements were made for the creation of a new civilian police force to take over responsibility for public security. All this, claimed the FMLN, represented a historic victory for the nation as a whole, rather than for one particular side. In the opinion of some FMLN leaders, the negotiation process had not only ended the war, but had brought about a 'democratic revolution' in which military confrontation was to be replaced by political conflict within the framework of parliamentary democracy.

Today, nearly two years after Chapultepec, El Salvador remains a contradictory mixture of hope and resignation, optimism and frustration. The only visible traces of the war in the capital are the numerous armless or legless youths begging or hobbling around on crutches, and the graffiti left over from a vanished revolutionary era – the inevitable 'Yankees out' interspersed with slogans calling for national independence and self-determination and lists of some of El Salvador's most prominent martyrs. The army no longer patrols the streets but the national police are still a constant presence, their members as heavily armed as they were during the war. In theory, the national police should have already been dissolved and replaced by the new national civilian police, but both the process of dissolution and the deployment of the new force have been delayed in what many consider to be deliberate tactics by the ARENA government. In the past, the national police were considered to be little more than an extension of the armed forces, and many members of the dismantled national guard and treasury police are believed to have joined their ranks since the end of the war.

Nowadays, the main function of the national police is in the control of crime rather than counter-insurgency, but the use of torture and arbitrary violence against real or imagined delinquents continues to be common practice among many of its members. The blight of criminal violence which has spread across the country in the last two years is one of the most serious problems of the postwar period, with an average of eighty murders a month and armed robberies, assaults and hold-ups a daily occurrence in many parts of the country. Commando-style raids, carried out by paramilitary groups using methods and weaponry inherited from the war, have necessitated wartime security measures in banks and private businesses in the cities, and armed assaults on public buses have become commonplace, even in broad daylight. The high rate of criminality has unpredictable consequences in a still-polarised society which has barely begun to recover from twelve years of continuous armed conflict. Both the FMLN and the armed forces have accused each other of deliberately promoting criminal violence in order to destabilise the country. For the military and its supporters on the Right, the issue of *la delinquencia* has provided a further excuse to delay and even reverse the demilitarisation of Salvadoran society and give the army the responsibility for public security that it still hankers after. Last year, as crime rates soared all over the country, the government responded to the urgent demand for action from the population by deploying 3,000 soldiers on some of the main highways. Even though the army was forbidden to stop vehicles or carry out patrols away from the highways, the deployment was criticised by the Left as a breach of the Peace Accords. It was, nevertheless, extremely popular with the public, for whom the presence of the army was seen as a price worth paying in return for security.

Even though the issue of criminality has clearly been to the political advantage of the Right, there is no need to resort to conspiracy theories to explain the spread of lawlessness and criminality in Salvadoran society. Throughout the capital, the presence of beggars, street kids and sidewalk vendors provides graphic evidence of extreme poverty and deprivation. From the rich, walled-in houses in the exclusive Escalón district to the impoverished slums that surround the city, San Salvador remains a city divided by invisible frontiers of wealth and power. As a result of the flight of peasants from the countryside during the war, the urban population of El Salvador has passed 50 per cent for the first time in its history. The impact of rural migration to the cities has been particularly dramatic in San Salvador itself, where the 1986 earthquake compounded the city's problems in absorbing internal refugees and people displaced by the war. Whether they came in search of employment or simply to escape the war in the countryside, the majority of the new arrivals ended up in shantytowns around the city, building precarious, makeshift shelters in neighbourhoods without water, electricity or sanitation.

Soyapango and Segundo Montes

The '16th March' community is part of Soyapango, one of the poorest districts of the capital, with a large number of displaced people and internal refugees. Like many areas of Soyapango, the community came into existence as the result of a mass occupation of public land in 1990, when eighty-four families squatted land belonging to the city council. Since then, the inhabitants of '16th March' have been engaged in a continuous struggle to prevent eviction and pressure the authorities into providing basic services. The community is pro-FMLN and highly politicised, and the neat, mudbrick houses and well-kept streets testify to a level of organisation that is frequently absent in other areas of Soyapango. Yet the settlement remains without many basic services and the threat of eviction is always a possibility. A large number of its inhabitants are single women, who are either unemployed or work in the 'informal sector' selling sweets, fruit and cigarettes in the city centre.

In the wilder fringes of neo-liberal thought, the hundreds of female street vendors thronging the sidewalks of San Salvador, with their children in cardboard boxes beside them, form part of the new breed of entrepreneurs who are expected to revitalise the Latin American economy in the future. Beyond this mercantile fantasy world, the reality is somewhat different. In San Salvador, as elsewhere, the majority of the city's street vendors live a precarious existence from one day to the next, without ever accumulating the capital or savings necessary to start their own businesses and enter 'the market'. The Salvadoran NGO, Procumes, an alternative development organisation which works closely with the marginalised communities in the capital, has attempted to remedy this situation through the promotion of small, collectively-run businesses, such as the small co-operative bakery in '16th March'. The bakery is presently providing training to nine women from the community and is expected to become profitable within the next few months. 'Our main aim is to generate income and promote self-sufficiency', explained Procumes worker Oscar, 'but we want to do it with collective models of organisation which oppose the neo-liberal individualist model. We need projects in which the people themselves participate in the taking of decisions and the execution of the projects.'

The policy of generating income in marginalised or displaced communities formed part of the developmental strategy of the Left during the war, and the reduction in economic aid since the end of the conflict has intensified the need to find alternative economic models which provide a living to the most vulnerable sectors of the population. Yet the task of alleviating poverty has been made more difficult by the structural adjustment programme imposed on El Salvador by the IMF and the World Bank, which has increased unemployment and led to a further reduction in the living standards of the poor. In the three years since the ARENA government began to liberalise the Salvadoran economy along the lines dictated by the international financial institutions, the price of subsistence foodstuffs such as beans, corn and flour have soared, while salaries have fallen or remained the same. The fall in real wages and the increased cost of living have forced many poor families to reduce their daily food intake while, at the same time, powerful agribusiness sectors close to ARENA have made big profits through speculation and hoarding of foodstuffs and the export of staple subsistence crops such as beans for sale abroad. The projects sponsored by the governmental Social Investment Fund (FIS) have failed to cushion the impact of structural adjustment, and the privatisation of the state sector has resulted in mass sackings of workers, pushing national unemployment figures well beyond the official figure of 35 per cent.

The impact of international monetary fundamentalism on El Salvador has not provided the most favourable conditions for the kind of alternative development projects and collectivist forms of organisation traditionally favoured by the Left, especially since international economic aid to the country is increasingly being channelled directly through the government. Nor is the commitment to collective forms of organisation a universal demand within the Left itself. 'It is necessary to break with paternalism, forced collectivisation and egalitarianism,' Joachín Villalobos, the general secretary of the People's Revolutionary Army (ERP), has written. The brilliant young commander of the Morazán front during the war, Villalobos has become the main theoretician for progressive capitalism within the FMLN. Earlier this year, the ERP proclaimed its conversion from revolutionary socialism to social democracy and changed its name to the cryptic 'People's Renovative Expression'. The ERP has gone further down the road than the other four organisations in the FMLN in jettisoning its socialist ideology and in claiming that 'freedom of expression, political democracy and free competition should be carried through to their ultimate consequences'. In its electoral manifesto and in numerous statements by its leaders, however, the FMLN as a whole appears to have accepted that it must operate within a capitalist framework for the foreseeable future and is concentrating its efforts on the creation of a 'popular economic bloc', which is both favourable to the Left and able to compete in a capitalist market. To this end, all the five organisations within the FMLN have established profit-making enterprises, ranging from agricultural co-ops and import-export companies, to the conversion of the legendary guerrilla radio station, Radio Venceremos, into a commercial radio station in which ideology and politics have been replaced by non-stop Latin pop and inane DJ patter.

Whether the discovery of venture capitalism by former guerrilla commanders owes more to economic necessity than ideological conviction, it has little to do with socialism either. Like the Latin American Left in general, the FMLN is undergoing a period of profound ideological redefinition in which fundamental goals and strategies on a whole range of issues are being called into question, including the role of the United States, the political strategy for the elections and the nature of the socialist project itself. As a result of this process, many political and economic tenets traditionally associated with the Left have been discarded, such as the call for nationalisation which formed part of the FMLN's 1980 manifesto. 'We can't oppose privatisation', explained one left-wing trade unionist in justification of the new realism:

> The basis of the economy in El Salvador is private property. We can't change that. What we are saying is that if you have to have privatisation, then we should try to reduce its impact on the workforce and the level of unemployment, and increase the participation of the workforce in the newly-privatised industries. We are only opposed to the exclusivist model of privatisation, in which wealth remains in the same few hands.

The problem, as the same trade unionist admitted, is that privatisation is generally designed to ensure exactly that and El Salvador has been no exception. As a result of the privatisation of the banks under the Cristiani government, a handful of traditionally dominant families from the oligarchy have regained the control of the country's financial system that they lost in the early 1980s, and the privatisation process has generally favoured the elite financial sectors at the expense of the workers.

All this has drastically reduced the capacity of the Left to act on behalf of the poorest sectors of the population, even as it tries to balance the conflicting demands of competition within the capitalist market with a commitment to social justice. The largest and most well-known of the alternative development projects in El Salvador is Segundo Montes, a community of 8,000 former refugees in the department of Morazán. The community was established under the auspices of the ERP, with whom it is still closely associated, when refugees living in camps in Honduras made a mass return to Morazán in the late 1980s. During their exile in Honduras, the refugees had learned new skills and founded carpentry and mechanical workshops with the help of aid and assistance from international solidarity. On their return to Morazán, they brought with them the production units they had founded in the refugee camps, in order to provide the new settlement with an economic base whose profits would be used for the benefit of the whole community, in the form of services and housing. The decision to establish Segundo Montes in the heart of the war zone was an extremely courageous one and reflected the idealism and political commitment of the campesinos who formed the majority of the population. Today, however, the utopian vision of self-sufficiency and social justice has begun to founder in the face of continued poverty and mass unemployment within the community. In addition, Segundo Montes is in the throes of a bitter dispute between the leadership of the community and the workers in the production units, which threatens the whole future of the project.

The immediate cause of the dispute can be traced to the decision by some of the workers to convert their production units into co-operatives in order to achieve greater efficiency and productivity. This decision was opposed by the leadership council on the grounds that the profits of each production centre belong to the whole community and that the breakaway workers were attempting to monopolise community resources for themselves. The workers, on the other hand, have refuted the charge, accusing the leadership of corruption, mis-management and authoritarianism.

Whether the charges of corruption are true or not, there is no doubt that the central committee has reacted with extraordinary hostility to these manifestations of autonomy from the workforce and has shown itself extremely reluctant to engage in democratic debate on the way the community should be managed. Since the dispute came out into the open last year, the leadership has carried out a relentless defamatory campaign against the *cooperativistas* and their supporters, which has done it little credit. Not only have workers been sacked for belonging to the new union established by the *cooperativistas*, but the leadership has used the community radio station and even the national press to make threats and false accusations against them. Last year, the leadership sacked four Irish volunteers sympathetic to the new union and appealed to the Ministry of the Interior to have them deported. When I asked a repre-sentative of the leadership council why these volunteers had been sacked, I was told that they had originally been hired as technical advisers but they had 'got involved in politics' and begun 'dividing people'.

In the official view of the leadership, the dispute is solely due to the selfishness of a group of workers who have been manipulated by foreign outsiders and drawn into 'politics'. Later that day, in a small room in the mechanical workshop used as a meeting place by the new union, the ATM, workers gave a very different version of the dispute, complaining of low wages and intimidation from factory foremen, lack of democracy and accountability from the leadership and the handing out of jobs and housing by prominent community leaders in exchange for political loyalty. 'I fought for the FMLN because I believed in social justice,' said an ATM organiser called Mario; 'before, I carried a gun, now I debate. We won the Peace Accords for the whole nation, but here in this community there are people who have lost the revolutionary vision that we fought for and become corrupted, and we have to stand up to them too.'

So great is the animosity and distrust generated by the dispute that it is difficult to imagine the ATM and the leadership achieving a modus vivendi, although negotiations between the two groups are being planned for the near future. It is to be hoped that a negotiated solution can be found, since a split in the community would be disastrous, not only for its population, but for similar projects elsewhere in the country for whom Segundo Montes is something of a model.

Among other things, the dispute in Segundo Montes has demonstrated the need for real democratic reform within the Left and has shown that a population prepared to accept low wages and a military command structure during the war is not necessarily prepared to do so in peacetime. During the twelve years of armed conflict, the close relationship between the ERP leadership and the civilian population of Morazán was parallelled in other parts of the country controlled by the FMLN. Since the end of the war, however, the links between the Frente and its rural base of support have been weakened, as middle and upper level cadres have moved to the capital to carry out political tasks on behalf of their respective organisations and prepare for the elections. The transformation of the FMLN from a clandestine politico-military organisation into a political party, with a national presence capable of challenging ARENA, has been difficult enough in itself, but it has been further complicated by the additional responsibilities of ensuring that the Peace Accords are kept. All this has demanded a new deployment of resources and personnel, which has tended to marginalise the desperate situation of the ex-combatants and the civilian populations in the former zones of conflict.

Chalatenango

Throughout the war, the mountains of Chalatenango provided the FMLN with one of its most secure bases, in spite of constant bombardments and military assaults. It was in Chalatenango that more than 600 peasants were slaughtered while fleeing army helicopters at the beginning of the war. Thousands more campesinos were driven across the border into Honduras or fled to the town of Chalatenango in the same period, leaving entire villages and hamlets deserted or destroyed by aerial and mortar bombardments as the army attempted to 'drain the sea' which supported the guerrillas. From the mid-1980s onwards, refugees began to return to the area en masse, repopulating their original villages or occupying others which had been left abandoned. Today, some of these villages have been completely rebuilt, while others remain deserted or partially destroyed, grim monuments to the devastating impact of 'low-intensity war' on the civilian population. Traditionally one of the poorest and least-developed regions in the country, communications in the former guerrilla zone in Chalatenango are poor, and horses are a more common means of transport on these pot-holed, unpaved roads than the occasional buses or pickups. At the end of the rainy season, the mountains are covered with banana trees and luxuriant green vegetation, interspersed with the tiny plots of land or *milpas* where the campesinos grow their staple maize crop. In the repopulated village of Las Vueltas, a fiesta is in progress to celebrate the sixth anniversary of the formation of the community and the streets are decked out with colourful streamers. Only the military boots and camouflage trousers worn by many inhabitants of the village provide evidence of the war – along with the 500lb bomb placed as a permanent monument next to the church, bearing the message, 'this is the peace the government and the armed forces are offering our communities'.

Like most of the villages in Chalatenango, Las Vueltas was organised by the Popular Liberation Forces (FPL) and its affairs are still managed by the various elected committees which sprang up during the war to organise community health, education and economic production following the collapse of the state administration. The alternative power structures established by the FPL provided thousands of campesinos with their first-ever experience of self-government and community organisation. Nowadays, the local popular assemblies (PPLs), which acted as representative village councils during the war, are still functioning in many parts of Chalatenango but neither they nor the popular committees are recognised by the ARENA government as legitimate forms of administration. 'There isn't as much participation in the PPLs as there used to be during the war,' says Irma, an FPL member in her early 30s; 'people have lost their enthusiasm. There's a lot of discontent. During the war there was so much solidarity between us; now suddenly the whole thing is over and we don't know how to recreate the same spirit of collective work. In my opinion, the change from war to peace was just too abrupt. Too many people were just abandoned when the war ended. We should have found alternatives, so that we could have kept people together.'

Like thousands of other Salvadorans who joined the revolutionary movement, Irma became involved in politics through her work as a lay preacher, or catechist, in the late 1970s. Following the assassination of Archbishop Romero in 1980, she became an organiser with the FPL, working in close contact with the civilian population, both inside guerrilla-controlled territory and in the dangerous *zonas de expansión* where the FMLN had not taken control. Since the end of the war, she has continued to live inside the former guerrilla zone where she spent most of the war, carrying out work in health education in the villages. In the course of her work, she has observed at first hand the general disintegration in morale among the population and the growing incidence of alcoholism, robbery and even rape. The social disintegration of communities subject to strict codes of revolutionary morality during the war is not surprising, considering the bleak economic situation in Chalatenango, where the majority of campesinos are even poorer than they were at the start of the war. 'People expected the Peace Accords to bring about a complete change in their lives,' said Irma, 'instead they're in the same situation as before, or even worse. It's difficult to know what to say when old people who lost their children during the war come up to me in tears and ask me who is going to look after them in their old age, and what was the point of it all, and how is the Frente going to help them.'

In parts of Chalatenango, there have been reports of armed bandit groups consisting of ex-members of the FMLN and the armed forces, in an alarming parallel to the phenomenon of the rearmed groups in the north of Nicaragua. I asked Irma if she thought that the disillusionment and discontent among the local population could eventually take the form of spontaneous armed action with political objectives, as it had in Nicaragua. 'It's possible, although it hasn't happened yet. Even though many people feel abandoned by the Frente, there's always a little spark of hope in the FMLN, that perhaps things will get better after the elections, but we will have to change our methods if we want to keep their support. There isn't enough clarity from the leadership. People have become too used to just receiving orders from the top, and this makes them passive.'

The same sense of disillusionment and postwar discontent can be found in other former conflict zones as well. Only one and a half hours from the capital lies the legendary Cerro de Guazapa, one of the most heavily-bombed guerrilla zones of the war. Unable to enter the area without the massive deployment of troops, the military relied heavily on the air force to bludgeon the population into submission. In spite of the unbelievably harsh conditions in which the FMLN and its civilian supporters lived and fought, 'Guazapa *heroica*' remained under guerrilla control for the duration of the war.

Today, the former guerrilla zone is reached by a twenty-minute walk from the pretty provincial town of Suchitoto. On my way out of the town, I walk with a campesino from one of the nearby villages, accompanied by his young son. During the war, he says, most of the surrounding land was occupied by campesinos loyal to the FMLN, following the flight of the landowners from the area at the beginning of the war. Now, some of the original landowners have come back and are trying to regain control of their former property. Under the terms of the Peace Accords, those landowners who have had their lands occupied must sell them to the banks and the land is then resold to the campesinos, who have thirty years to pay it off following a three-year grace period. This compromise arrangement has not been particularly popular with the campesinos, who believed that the land they had occupied and worked during the war now belonged to them forever. 'How did the original owners get their land anyway?' my companion asks. 'When the Spanish came here 500 years ago, they conned the people, giving the Indians beads and mirrors in exchange for their land. Anyway, if the party that everyone here supports wins the elections, we hope we won't have to pay.'

There is no need to ask which party he is referring to, since we are already well into the former guerrilla zone. After twenty minutes, we arrive in Aguacayo, the centre of 'heroic Guazapa', and pass the huge container where the guerrillas handed over thousands of weapons to the UN following the ceasefire. Twelve years of aerial bombardments and mortar attacks have reduced this former community of 2,000 to an eerie ghost town. Entire streets of gutted, pulverised houses are overgrown with vegetation, without roofs or windows. In some places, the cobbled streets are still visible; elsewhere, they have become completely overgrown. Outside the bombed-out church, where five campesinos were murdered by the national guard in 1980, a woman sells coca-cola to the few visitors who pass through the ruins, and a short distance away stands the former FMLN command post, where a mural has been painted to commemorate the signing of the Accords.

Amazingly, there are still seventeen families living amid the devastation, in the few houses that have been left more or less intact. Like the inhabitants of the other former guerrilla zones, they have received no help from the government since the war ended and the only assistance they have received has come from the church. 'The peace is good,' says Leopoldo, a member of the Aguacayo village committee; 'you can go out of your house without being afraid of being picked up by the national guard, but we need funds to be able to work. The land transfers haven't been organised well, most people haven't had their claims legalised yet.'

In spite of the fact that both ARENA and the FMLN agreed to take urgent steps to ensure the reintegration of ex-combatants from both sides into civilian life as soon as possible, only a tiny proportion of former combatants have received the land they were promised and the majority of those who have received land are still without the legal proof of ownership they need to obtain credit from the banks. Even if peasants like Leopoldo do eventually obtain legal title to the land, it is difficult to see how they are going to make their plots productive enough to pay back their mortgages and debts to the banks. In Nicaragua, the privatised banks have used their control of credit facilities to undermine peasant co-operatives and regain control of land that was redistributed by the Sandinistas. The same process could easily occur in El Salvador, in peasant communities dependent for their survival on external credit and financial support.

A few miles from Aguacayo lies the Ciudadela Guillermo Ungo, a group of nine small settlements of formerly displaced people, where the economic situation is little better. Originally established on the estate of a landowner who had fled to the capital, the 'city' of Guillermo Ungo was not part of the guerrilla zone during the war and the lush green countryside surrounding it was the scene of some of the heaviest fighting of the war. 'There were battles around here day and night,' says Julio, a young ex-combatant. 'There is hardly a family in the area that didn't lose a child or relative.'

Julio became a guerrilla at the age of 12, following the torture and murder of his father by one of the death squads. As we sit in front of the mountain range where he fought for twelve years, he describes the apocalyptic period just before the war, when the death squads terrorised the countryside on behalf of the landowners and the bodies of murdered peasants turned up on a daily basis in nearby Lake Ilopango. Faced with a virtual war of extermination against their organisations, the peasants fought back with stones, machetes and garrottes, gradually accumulating an arsenal with small arms and weapons taken from the enemy. 'That's how we did it,' Julio says pointedly, 'not with weapons from Cuba.'

That these irregular forces, composed mostly of untrained campesinos, were able to fight the Salvadoran armed forces and their US backers to a draw is an astonishing achievement, of which ex-fighters like Julio are justly proud. Now that the war has ended, however, the young veterans of Guillermo Ungo find themselves facing a future which offers little or no prospect of a short-term improvement in their lives. 'Right now we're worse off than we were during the war,' says Julio; 'we have nothing, no houses, no land, no work. There are people in the FMLN who get salaries and cars and didn't even fight in the war, while I was here fighting the whole time. I know that everybody has different tasks in a war, but I wish the Frente would give me some help. When I began the war I was in fourth grade. That doesn't prepare you for anything. I wish the Frente would give me some help to go on studying.'

Given the limited financial resources that the FMLN has at its disposal, such aspirations are unlikely to be fulfilled in the near future. Along with many communities in the former conflict zones, the inhabitants of Guillermo Ungo received limited quantities of international aid during the war, which have either been stopped or reduced in the last two years. Even though the majority of international aid is now being channelled through the ARENA government, the Cristiani administration has shown little inclination to provide assistance to its former enemies and the lion's share of state reconstruction investment has been directed towards infrastructural improvements that favour the business community, instead of emergency aid to the devastated communities in the former war zones.

The failure of the government to fulfil its social obligations cannot be attributed to irrational political malice alone. In the last two years, some of the landowners have begun to return to Guazapa and many of them have been extremely reluctant to sell their land to the banks and legalise the transfer to their new occupants. Not only has the ARENA government made no attempt to pressure them, but it has failed to make the necessary funds available which the banks need to make the purchases. 'A lot of people here feel very insecure,' explained a

Lutheran church volunteer working with the Guillermo Ungo community. 'They are working on lands that they don't have titles for, which they don't know if they'll be able to keep. Many people are afraid that if ARENA win the elections, they'll be evicted by force.'

The tension in Guillermo Ungo is a reflection of the larger, unresolved conflict between campesinos who have taken part in a revolutionary process and a reactionary rural elite eager to reassert its power and authority in the postwar era. Given the evictions that have already taken place in other parts of the country, and the deep-rooted hostility of the Salvadoran ruling class towards any notion of land reform or redistribution of wealth, the fears of a right-wing political offensive in the countryside following an ARENA electoral victory are by no means unfounded. At the same time, such a course of action would be fraught with dangers and could not be easily accomplished. Too many campesinos have suffered repression at the hands of ARENA and its supporters to allow themselves to be dispossessed without a struggle. 'If the big landowners had carried out reforms in the first place, there wouldn't have been a war,' said a member of Guillermo Ungo's village committee. 'ARENA are the owners of the country and they controlled the killers and the death squads. The shooting has stopped but the war isn't over, and we will show them that our people still have power.'

Morazán

The conflict between the old rural elites and the alternative communities established in the zones of conflict is made even more complex by the population displacement that took place during the war. Many of the present inhabitants now living in the former war zones have taken over not only lands, but houses and villages abandoned by their original owners at the beginning of the conflict. One example of the problems that this situation has engendered is the village of Perquín, the former 'guerrilla capital' of Morazán. Set amid pine-covered mountains near the Honduran border, this tranquil rural village was the ERP's wartime base of operations in the Morazán front. Despite countless bombardments, artillery and mortar attacks and military assaults, the army was never able to dislodge the guerrillas and secure the village.

As a result of the fierce fighting in and around Perquín, the social composition of the village was totally changed, with the richer inhabitants moving to the nearby town of San Francisco Gotera, while the poorer peasants from the surrounding countryside moved into the village to take advantage of the relative protection offered by the FMLN. The exiled inhabitants continued to vote in the general and local elections that took place during the war and the result is that Perquín now has a Christian Democrat mayor, elected by the exiled minority, in spite of the fact that the majority of the population in the village is pro-FMLN. Since the end of the war, the mayor has returned to Perquín to take up a legal position which bears no relation to the actual political orientation of the village, and relations between the new administration and the FMLN and its supporters in the village have been marked by mutual animosity and suspicion. To make matters worse, the mayor is widely believed to be an ARENA puppet, spearheading an attempt by the exiled population and the extreme Right to reassert their power in a historic guerrilla base which is now the site of the first museum of the Salvadoran revolution.

In 1993, the antagonism between the two groups reached a crisis point over the new administration's decision to demolish a bombarded building in the main square. The building was the site of the mayor's office before the war and the administration wants to rebuild the new mayoralty in the same place, while the FMLN wants to preserve part of the ruins as a war memorial. In September, the dispute nearly turned violent when a large group of FMLN supporters forcibly prevented the mayor and his construction crew from knocking down the building. The pro-ARENA press predictably seized on the confrontation as a typical example of the lawless, undemocratic behaviour of the FMLN mob, without explaining the political background behind it. In the opinion of Father Rogelio Ponseele, the priest of Perquín, the issue of the mayoralty is being used as a test of strength by the wealthier exiles who are trying to return to Perquín. 'If the mayor wanted to, he could easily build his office in another part of the village, but he and his supporters are trying to demonstrate their power over the popular organisations here. They want to show that they can do this as a first step, and then they want to evict people from their homes and take back their lands.'

A ruddy-faced Belgian in his mid-fifties, Father Rogelio is an admirer of Martin Luther King and has spent more than twenty years in El Salvador. At the beginning of the war, he was invited by the ERP to work with the Christian base communities in the area. The contribution of priests, nuns and lay preachers was vital to the development of the revolutionary movement in El Salvador, and liberation theology was particularly influential in Morazán, where thousands of campesinos received their ideological inspiration, not from Marx, but from the bible, and joined the base communities like the one in Perquín, which fought alongside the organisations of the Left. 'When I first came here, the ERP told me the war would only last a few months,' says Father Rogelio. 'At that time we thought we were going to change everything. Instead, I was here for twelve years with the people. When I look back on the fear, hunger and insecurity of those years, I don't know how we managed to stand it.' The fact that so much suffering did not end in a popular victory has not diminished the utopian aspirations of the base communities, but the end of the war has brought new priorities in their work with the local population, with an emphasis on education, health care and personal relationships. 'We are living in hope', Father Rogelio explained, 'rather than euphoria. We have important political spaces that we never had before, but the real achievements of the Peace Accords aren't visible yet. The country is only at the beginning of a new phase in its history and the Accords are our political tools.'

In spite of his cautious optimism, Father Rogelio has few illusions about the nature of ARENA and the Salvadoran Right. 'There are a few people on the Right who are sensitive to the changes that have taken place and are prepared to make compromises, but in general the Right in this country is feudal, reactionary and recalcitrant. They want peace, but a peace based on a return to the past.'

The extreme Right's domination of Salvadoran politics throughout most of the century has always ensured the most violent response to any popular demand for change or reform, from the infamous *matanza* of 1931 to the bloody repression of the popular organisations in the late seventies. A few miles from Perquín lie the ruins of El Mozote, the site of one of the most horrendous crimes of the war. In this area, in December 1981, an estimated 1,000 unarmed campesinos believed to be sympathetic to the FMLN were systematically murdered by the US-trained Atlacatl battalion, during a two-day military operation. The majority of the victims were women and children, who were killed in the most sadistic fashion in an act of gratuitous savagery that the then Reagan administration described as a propaganda stunt by the guerrillas. Today, the foundations of the little church, where more than a hundred children were burned alive by the 'angels of death' of the Atlacatl, can still be seen. All that is left of the rest of the village are a few charred concrete buildings, overgrown with vegetation, and four silhouettes of a family holding hands to symbolise the community that once lived there.

It is not known whether President Cristiani was referring to El Mozote when he told a triumphal gathering of soldiers on Armed Forces Day in 1992 that 'your glorious deeds will live forever in the annals of Salvadoran history'. What is certain, however, is that in May 1993, only four days after the publication of the Truth Commission report implicating the armed forces in a range of crimes and atrocities, including El Mozote, Cristiani declared a general amnesty for all those accused of war crimes, in order to 'bury this painful chapter in our country's history'. Such magnanimity might have been more impressive had it come from the relatives of the victims, rather than from ARENA, the party formed by the deceased torturer and death squad organiser, Roberto d'Aubuisson. While there are sectors of Salvadoran society, such as the Catholic church, that have expressed their willingness to forgive those involved in war crimes following a public clarification of the truth, it was never argued that the executioners had the right to forgive themselves. Whether the amnesty was a voluntary initiative from ARENA itself, or the result of pressure from the armed forces, it was nevertheless a gesture of supreme contempt towards the Truth Commission and the survivors and witnesses who testified in the belief that justice would finally be done.

The continued influence of the extreme Right over government policy was further demonstrated by the long delay in retiring the notorious 'class of 65' officers who directed the armed forces during the war and the failure to carry out other recommendations made by the Truth Commission, such as the purging of the corrupt judiciary and a thorough investigation into the death squads. Although Cristiani was finally forced by international pressure to carry out the changes in the military high command in June, the government has ignored criticism of the amnesty. Once again, as in many other Latin American countries undergoing transitions from dictatorship, the cooperation of the military appears to have been achieved through behind-the-scenes agreements which relegate crimes against humanity to historical oblivion.

Crime, democracy and the peace process

In spite of the initial public outcry that greeted the amnesty in May, there has been little pressure since from either the FMLN or the Salvadoran population as a whole to bring perpetrators of war crimes to trial. The FMLN's room for manoeuvre in this issue is somewhat limited by the fact that some of its own members, including Joachín Villalobos himself, were accused by the Truth Commission of involvement in human rights abuses, however minimal in comparison with those of the armed forces. In general, public opinion is divided between those who believe that the trial and punishment of war criminals is politically impossible, however morally desirable, and those who believe that justice is a political and moral imperative for the whole nation, on which the future of Salvadoran democracy depends. It is also clear, in spite of the condemnation from the international community that accompanied the amnesty, that neither the UN nor the US government has any intention of pursuing the issue any further.

While there is no doubt that an attempt to bring army officers to trial would provoke a major political crisis, it is equally certain that a viable democracy cannot be constructed on the basis of historical amnesia, especially when the same forces responsible for state terrorism in the past are still active within Salvadoran society. Since the signing of the ceasefire, approximately 280 FMLN members are reported to have died in unexplained circumstances across the country. While these statistics do not approach the thousands of demobilised guerrillas who have been killed in Colombia, they are still extremely serious.

Until October 1993, the majority of these killings involved low-level members of the FMLN and the left-of-centre opposition. Often the assassinations were clumsily disguised as criminal attacks to hide the political motivation behind them, while others bore the unmistakable hallmarks of the death squads. On the eve of the election campaign in October, however, three former FMLN commanders were killed in one ten-day period, two of them in clear death squad attacks. The killings brought swift condemnation from the US government and the UN peacekeeping force in El Salvador, forcing Cristiani to announce an investigation into the death squads for the first time. Since the financial support for the death squads is long believed to have come from within the Salvadoran oligarchy, which ARENA represents, it is difficult to believe that the investigation will be carried through. The choices facing the government were further complicated the following month, when declassified CIA papers appeared in the US press, directly implicating the ARENA presidential and vice-presidential candidates for the next elections in acts of right-wing terrorism in the early 1980s.

The crisis over the assassinations demonstrated once again the fragility of the political consensus in El Salvador and the extent to which national reconciliation is still dependent on the intervention of outside actors. Again and again, at crucial moments during and after the negotiations, the intervention of the United Nations or the US government has prevented the dialogue between the two sides from collapsing. The permanent presence of the UN observation team in El Salvador has had a decisive influence on the peace process and its role has been highly praised by the FMLN leadership.

At the same time, the very fact that the peace process has been so dependent on external pressures raises doubts as to what will happen in El Salvador once the international presence in the country is removed in the wake of the elections. The US policy of promoting demilitarisation in El Salvador reflects the change in its geopolitical priorities in the post-Cold War era, rather than any sudden concern for the welfare of the Salvadoran population. For more than thirty years, successive US governments favoured the rule of the armed forces and the strengthening of the 'national security state' as the most reliable bulwarks against 'international communism' in El Salvador. Not until the early 1980s did the Reagan administration belatedly discover democracy as a counter-insurgency tactic to isolate the FMLN, in conjunction with free-fire zones and bombings of the civilian population. In the era of GATT and the TLC, with the popular movements in Central America defeated or neutralised, US policy is directed towards regional stability and the restructuring of national economies along neo-liberal lines, and this has resulted in a decline in both military and economic aid to the region at precisely the time when reconstruction funds are most needed.

For those social forces within El Salvador seeking a genuine participatory democracy with some measure of social justice, therefore, the United States is an extremely unreliable ally. Even as the US government continues to promote demilitarisation, US troops have taken part in 'civic aid' projects with both the Salvadoran and Guatemalan armies. The continued influence of far-Right US politicians over US policy towards the Sandinistas is an indication of the kind of treatment that the FMLN can expect from its former enemies in the future, for all its new-found pretension to 'respectability'.

The fickle interest of the US and the 'international community' leaves the demobilised FMLN and the popular movement in a dangerously vulnerable position, should the armed forces and the Right go on the offensive. As one FMLN militant in Chalatenango told me, 'In the past, when there was work or political demands, the political struggle was in the streets, strong, massive and secure, but what supported it? A revolutionary army that no longer exists. So what many people are asking is, how are we going to make sure the government fulfils its obligations? If we don't have an armed force at our disposal, then what power do we really have?'

Much political capital was made by the Right over the FMLN's supposed 'bad faith' in 1993, following the explosion of a large FPL arms cache in Managua. Yet most UN military observers affirm that the majority of remaining FMLN arms deposits consist of deteriorated and useless weapons. Less attention has been paid to the large stocks of weapons distributed by the military to its paramilitary allies during the war, most of which are still unaccounted for. And in May 1993, police and soldiers demonstrated their commitment to national reconciliation by opening fire on a peaceful demonstration of blind and disabled veterans from both the FMLN and the armed forces.

Such actions demonstrate that El Salvador is still a long way from the 'democratic revolution' heralded by Villalobos and cast some doubt on the durability of the peace process itself. The failure of the government to address the problems of postwar reconstruction, the Cristiani administration's hysterical opposition to last year's health workers' strike, and the recent withdrawal of business representatives from the Forum for Economic and Social Consensus, all demonstrate the brittle nature of the national consensus embodied in the Peace Accords. Even apart from the immediate problems of postwar reconstruction, El Salvador remains a country with enormous economic, social and ecological problems, most of which stem directly from the unequal distribution of land and wealth and the domination of the agro-export elite throughout the last century. Population pressure has further limited the economic resources available, leaving emigration as the only means of survival for growing numbers of Salvadorans.

Ultimately, the success of the peace process in El Salvador will depend on a resolution of the same socio-economic issues which led to the war in the first place, and so, too, will the attainment of any meaningful democracy. Without concrete improvements in the living standards of the population, the fragile consensus in the country could still be eroded in the future and political conflict could once more degenerate into violence. Even after the war, El Salvador remains one of the most unstable and dangerous societies in Latin America in terms of criminal violence.

Prior to the elections, many observers believed an ARENA victory to be the most likely possibility, with a possible majority for the FMLN-Convergencia coalition in parliament. Some even predicted a split in the FMLN in the wake of an electoral defeat, with the ERP breaking away to form a separate party.

The dissolution of the Frente would be an ironic consequence of the democratic transition which it helped to bring about, but it may well be inevitable, considering the internal conflicts within the organisation. In an article published shortly before his death, the murdered Jesuit intellectual Ignacio Ellacuria identified the abandonment by the Left of its utopian aspirations as one of the factors that had made a negotiated solution to the war a possibility. This transition has not been without its political cost for the FMLN, however, and the compromises it was forced to make have not been popular with all its members. Yet at no time did I meet or hear of anyone on the Salvadoran Left who had been against the negotiation process or supported a continuation of the war. Whether the democratic reforms won through the Peace Accords turn out to be permanent or not, they do represent a kind of victory for the popular movement, and the only real hope for Salvadoran society is that they can be strengthened and extended. 'We have lost nothing, because we had nothing,' Villalobos has written. 'On the contrary, we have won, because we have instruments of power and spaces to widen that power.'

It remains to be seen whether these 'instruments of power' will be strong enough to resist the inevitable attempts of the Right to recover its lost ground, or whether the entire negotiation process will turn out to be a brief lull in the long-running war between the army and the civil population. At the same time, the military and the Right would be unwise to push too hard. A generation of Salvadorans has passed through the crucible of war and revolution, who now have political and military skills that they did not have before, as the military has learned to its cost. As one cultural worker from Chalatenango explained, 'The army is beginning to understand its new role, which is to coexist alongside the population. They have the capacity to carry out a coup but it doesn't suit them, partly because of the international condemnation it would receive, but also because they know the people wouldn't accept it. They know that there is an army already formed among the people, without weapons or uniforms, but which is ready to act.'

January 1994

Postscript

The first elections in Salvadoran history to include all representative political forces ended on 24 April with an overwhelming victory for ARENA presidential candidate, Armando Calderon Sol. Despite his recently publicised involvement in right-wing terrorist activities in the early 1980s, Calderon Sol gained 68 per cent of the vote, compared with the 32 per cent obtained by the FMLN/Convergencia candidate, Ruben Zamora. Calderon Sol's predictable triumph followed earlier ARENA victories in the parliamentary and municipal elections in March, and confirmed ARENA as the dominant political force in the country, with thirty-nine out of eighty-four MPs, and 262 town councils. In its first-ever election, the FMLN/Convergencia coalition gained twenty-one seats, surpassing the Christian Democrats to become the second political force in the country, despite losing to ARENA in former guerrilla bases in Chalatenango and Morazán.

Although there was no evidence of the massive vote-rigging and intimidation of voters which characterised previous Salvadoran elections, these, the first since the end of the civil war, cannot be considered an exemplary model of democratic procedures. Over one million Salvadoran voters were not eligible to vote, as a result of bureaucratic inertia on the part of the Supreme Electoral Tribunal (TSE), and UN observers criticised the Tribunal for various irregularities, such as the lack of information made available to the population and a number of unexplained gaps in the electoral census. In a bizarre throwback to the past, a ballot-box full of votes mysteriously appeared in the hall where TSE magistrates were preparing to announce the electoral count to the press. The TSE also rejected all thirty-seven complaints made by the FMLN concerning electoral irregularities, while accepting the single complaint made by ARENA.

In spite of these irregularities and the notable lack of neutrality from the TSE, the FMLN has accepted the result; with some FMLN leaders even presenting its twenty-one seats as a relative success, given the Frente's short history as a political party and ARENA's huge financial resources. At the same time, the high rates of absenteeism (49 per cent and 55 per cent respectively in the two electoral rounds) provide irrefutable evidence of the failure of the 'elections of the century' to make a significant impact on the Salvadoran population. Given the FMLN's much-repeated claim to be acting as a catalyst for the democratic transformation of Salvadoran society as a whole, rather than a vanguard party on behalf of a particular class, the fact that over half the population declined to vote at all can hardly be considered encouraging. Once again, as in other Latin American countries in the process of demilitarisation, the foundations of democracy are being constructed without the active participation of the majority of the population. From the point of view of ARENA, the lack of genuine popular legitimacy is of secondary importance, now that its objective of maintaining itself in power has been achieved. For the FMLN, however, which has consistently described the Peace Accords as a victory for 'civil society', the apathetic response of the civilian population must be seen as a major setback to its political project. Absenteeism apart, the overwhelming ARENA victory will undoubtedly give further encouragement to the intransigent sectors on the Right represented by Calderon Sol himself. Already, in spite of the new President's election promise 'to govern for all Salvadorans', the government has announced the indefinite postponement of the dissolution of the national police (scheduled to reach completion in August 1994).

Further attempts to brake or reverse the political transformation of the country will certainly follow, especially when the presence of foreign observers is removed. As former guerrilla commanders take their place in parliament for the first time, it remains to be seen whether the FMLN can maintain the necessary unity to ensure the full implementation of the Peace Accords and hold back the inevitable political counteroffensive from the Right. But whether the Frente remains together or not, the future of the Salvadoran Left over the next five years will be decided by its ability to use the political spaces it has won to build on its traditional base and provide a national alternative to ARENA, while finding practical solutions to the disastrous economic circumstances in which the majority of the population are forced to live. The task of winning the support of a populace exhausted by years of war and disillusioned with politics and politicians of all stripes will not be an easy one, but the elections have clearly demonstrated that it cannot be achieved by electoral pragmatism alone. The more the FMLN tries to occupy the centre, the more it risks being 'routinised', and eventually surpassed by the Christian Democrats in the future. In the late 1970s, the Left succeeded in mobilising thousands of peasants, students and workers in a movement of political and social protest that eventually assumed revolutionary dimensions. Today, circumstances both inside and outside El Salvador have changed drastically, but if the Left is to provide a meaningful alternative for the Salvadoran poor and dispossessed, it must find ways to recover the idealism and moral force which were once its greatest strengths and demonstrate that democracy has more to offer than elections every five years.

References

1 Press interview, 1980.
2 This and all other Villalobos quotations are taken from *Una Revolución Democrática para una Revolución en la Izquierda* (1993).

STEVE VIEUX

In the shadow of
neo-liberal racism

One of the peculiarities of the current period is the one-sided
polarisation of social theory. On the one hand, neo-liberal social theory
offers a vigorous and confident defence of the capitalist social order.
This theory reflects the world-wide, rightward political turn. There has
been an elaboration and popularisation of neo-liberal social theory,
which amounts to a critique of existing capitalist society from capitalist
first principles. It is a total critique which brings every sphere of social
life before the bar of market rationality, from the organisation and
functioning of groups in civil society to the functioning of the institutions of representative democracy, to schools and universities. This
complex of theories, in all its ramifications, aims to promote and justify
inequality, to block interference with the market and ultimately to divide
and weaken the antagonists of the unfettered market mechanism.

On the other hand, neo-liberal social theory does not confront, or no
longer confronts, a theoretical antagonist equipped with a vigorous,
systemic critique of the capitalist order from the Left. On the contrary,
the mainspring of contemporary critical thought is postmodern social
theory. Journals with this particular emphasis proliferate, while many
established journals of the Left more and more open their pages to the
theory. Those that resist suffer the consequences. Can anyone doubt that
Social Text is more widely read today in the US than *Monthly Review*?
Postmodern theory specifically rejects any systemic theoretical critique
which would criticise capitalist social relations as an obstacle to human
emancipation. Critiques of this sort are dismissed as obsolete humanist

Steve Vieux is in the department of sociology, State University of New York,
Binghamton.

Race & Class, 36, 1 (1994)

confections which overlook the various and diverse, specific sites in which subjectivities are precariously constructed. Marxism becomes one more tired option on the theoretical menu; one more outmoded meta-narrative urging liberation. Yet it is not Marxism, but postmodern social theory which is outmoded in its refusal intellectually to confront either the deepening social polarisation facing US society, or neo-liberal theory, the prime intellectual defender of this trend.

Neo-liberal theory and practice

Neo-liberal theory so pervades the intellectual and political atmosphere that its presence may be overlooked. Of course, it begins with the celebration of the rationality of the market in the efficient allocation of resources. The functioning of the market must be protected from unwanted interlopers. In the neo-liberal mind, the chief potential interloper is the state itself. State intervention is inherently destructive and irrational, since the market is self-adjusting. It is an article of faith that state efforts to replace market activities will prove economically inefficient and harmful to human freedom.

In neo-liberal theory, parliamentary democracy in the west is the principal source of state intervention in the market. Parliaments have come to be endowed with entirely too much power. They ought to oversee the protection of the freedom of the individual through the elaboration and careful maintenance of the 'rule of law', the 'rules of just conduct', which apply equally to citizens. Parliaments ought not to confuse this task with the distribution of resources to satisfy particular, short-run ends of particular interest groups. The executive proper ought to devote itself to the allocation of resources for these purposes, on strictly technical and rational criteria, under the supervision of a parliament devoted to the rule of law. In the current arrangement, members of parliament misuse the resources available to bribe particular constituencies, in order to remain in power. They come to have a vested interest in exercising control over the broadest possible pool of resources, with the weakest possible limitations on its use. In Hayek's view, this is creeping totalitarianism.[1]

Thus, through a critique of parliamentarianism, neo-liberals are led inexorably to a critique of civil society itself, specifically of its organisations. It is these organisations which have turned parliamentary institutions into the 'playball of group interests', a 'bargaining democracy' subordinated to the short-run, egoistic concerns of the interest groups predominant in civil society. Though parliament hypocritically justifies its unrestrained powers by appeal to majority rule, the effect of log-rolling among interest groups must often prevent the political expression of majority opinion. Parliamentarians assemble majorities by cobbling together conglomerates of interest groups. As Hayek says, a parliament 'simply cannot confine itself to serving the agreed views of the majority of the electorate'.[2]

This critique of the proliferation of organised interest groups and their selfish search for brokered advantage refers specifically to 'the ubiquitous associations and unions of the different "trades"', and to the white-collar professions. Yet this critique does not apply to huge corporations or 'large productive units'. Nor does it apply to the selfishness of individuals, whose pursuit of their interests is largely in accord with the spontaneous market order.[3]

The effect of this growth of organisational power is to clog the free-flowing channels of market efficiency, blocking the process of constant innovation and adjustment which the market otherwise compels. 'All the benefits we receive from the spontaneous order of the market', Hayek says, 'are the results of such changes, and will be maintained only if the changes are allowed to continue. But every change of this kind will hurt some organised interests; and the preservation of the market order will therefore depend on those interests not being allowed to prevent what they dislike.'[4]

This is an impressive attack on western democracy, ranging over the whole of the society to make its critique and arriving at a truly radical condemnation of parliamentary democracy and its linkage with organised interest groups. The critique is a kind of pluralist theory with all the signs reversed. Now, the impact of interest groups on the state is not proof of the representative nature of western democracy, but of its corruption and illegitimacy. The network of group interests suborns parliament, falsifying majority opinion, threatening the integrity of market society and subverting fundamental freedoms.

The truly strange feature of this analysis is that it contains a theory of exploitation. Operating through the state, the selfish interest groups contrive to extract revenue from market society at large. As Hayek puts it:

> What is not yet generally recognized is that the real exploiters in our present society are not egotistic capitalists or entrepreneurs, and in fact not separate individuals, but organizations which derive their power from the moral support of collective action and the feeling of group loyalty.[5]

Exploitation is therefore expelled from the sphere of economics and production for the market and displaced into politics, where it serves as an obstacle to freedom and economic growth.

Of course, it is no secret that neo-liberal social theory fuelled the resurgence of the Right in US politics in a general sense, but the extent to which particular campaign themes within both the Republican and Democratic parties have, themselves, been lifted from this theory is itself especially noteworthy. One need only think of the attack on

Mondale as the defender of 'special interests', made within the Democratic Party by Gary Hart and by the Republicans in the general elections. The special interests that Mondale's critics had in mind were labour, African-Americans and feminists. When Mondale proposed an $85 billion tax hike, the door was opened for the brutal and effectively divisive application of Hayek's exploitation theory. The tax hike would be extracted from the generality of the population, as the Republicans portrayed it, and transferred to the 'special interests'.

This is how Reagan sounded the theme on the campaign stump:

> *Reagan:* 'Is there any doubt that they will raise our taxes?' *Audience:* 'No!' ... 'That they will make government bigger than ever?' 'No!' 'And deficits even worse?' 'No!' 'We're here to see that government continues to serve the people and not the other way around. Yes, government should do all that is necessary, but only that which is necessary. We don't lump people by groups or special interests.'[6]

Thus racialised for US campaigning, the neo-liberal dogma served as a powerful wedge for splitting the constituency of the Democratic Party on racial lines.

This same pattern was repeated again in the 1988 election by the Bush campaign. Bush and Atwater (Bush's key political adviser) linked Willie Horton* and Bush's tax pledge to create the same fundamental ideological configuration as in 1984, linking the supposed indulgence of the Democrats towards criminals, such as Horton, with their supposed fiscal indulgence towards African-Americans and other 'special interests'.[7]

The campaigning positions taken by Clinton in the last election were a not very subtle effort to elude the 'exploitation by taxes for the special interests' themes of the Right. Clinton avoided campaigning in the inner cities, held Jesse Jackson at arms' length and pledged to lower taxes on the 'middle class', while raising them on the rich. While escaping the typical Republican 'special interests' attack, he did so, in part, by avoiding the imagery and substance of African-American political concerns, as well as those of many other poor and working-class citizens. In this way, the continuing force of the 'special interest' charge was confirmed. If there is any doubt on this score, the mounting campaign by the Right around immigration issues should put it to rest. A principal theme in this agitation is that undocumented immigrants are using the state to siphon off far more in taxpayer-financed goods and services than they are contributing.[8]

Neo-liberal theory thus devised a totalising critique of capitalist

---

* Willie Horton was a black convict who, while allowed out on furlough, committed further crimes. The Bush campaign ran a nightly TV ad referring to Horton and featuring numbers of black men apparently leaving prison through a revolving door.

society from the Right, centred around a theory of exploitation. Far from merely offering an abstract and utopian scheme of the ideal market society and politics of the future, Hayek and the neo-liberals offer an ideological framework which has proven capable of doing real damage in the down-to-earth class politics of the western democracies.[9]

At the same time, the exploitation-by-interest-groups theme could be used for the purpose of explaining away the failures and cruelties of particular capitalist societies, putting them at the door of those who had suffered most under decaying US capitalism. One of the chief claims of the theory was that the demands of interest groups were choking off the sources of entrepreneurial creativity and vigour and diminishing the prosperity of the society as a whole. This theme could be presented in a nutshell in Reagan's call to 'get the government off the backs of the people', or in Mancur Olson's argument in *The Rise and Decline of Nations*.[10] Olson sought to devise a historical account of the growth and decay of capitalist societies, pointing to the density and durability of the organisation of interest groups as the key to long-run economic success or failure. This was a very clear, vigorously argued and reckless argument, which lent itself readily to scapegoating.

The postmodern alternative

While these ideas were sweeping campaign debates, rostrums and TV spots in the 1980s, the thought of such scholars as Michel Foucault, Jacques Derrida, Ernesto Laclau and Chantal Mouffe was sweeping through what remained of the Left, under the rubrics of post-modernism or post-structuralism, especially in the universities and colleges. The hallmark of this amorphous and difficult body of work is its insistence on the decentred character of social life. The latter is composed of congeries of discursive practices or micropowers, highly discrete and discontinuous, in which subjectivities are formed and re-formed. The whole business is so unstable, precarious and provisional that the word 'society' itself is called into question for lending a spurious unity and well-ordered coherence to social matters. 'Society', as Laclau and Mouffe proclaimed, 'is not a valid object of discourse.'[11] This assertion expresses their rejection of the idea of a structured social order.

For these thinkers, the state is simply one discursive practice among others, without any particular strategic or analytic priority.[12] For Foucault, the state is not a privileged instance of power. Such a conception he dismisses as a naive, juridical view of power:

> One impoverishes the question of power when one poses it uniquely in terms of legislation, or of the constitution, or only in terms of the state or state apparatus. Power is much more complicated, more dense and diffused than a set of laws or an apparatus of the state.[13]

One can hardly imagine an antagonist of neo-liberal theory less equipped to do battle with its ideas, in either theoretical or practical form. For the postmodernists, this is first of all a philosophical problem. Knowledge is reduced to an immediate expression of the power interests of competing subject positions. The production of knowledge becomes a simple ideological reflection of these positions, lacking its own methods of research, validation or verification. In this way, postmodernists find empirically-grounded research claims fundamentally uninteresting. Outrageous factual claims may be advanced without fear of refutation. The exploitation-by-special-interests argument rests on absurd assumptions about the extent to which the poor vote and participate in interest groups. We eagerly await a defence of the idea that the poor are somehow exploiting the rest of society, even while family income among the poor is falling, the minimum wage is degraded and welfare benefits fall.[14] The postmodern mood of hostility towards factual claim and counter-claim contributes to an intellectual atmosphere in which such absurdities can flourish.[15]

The insistence in this body of theory on the local and situational character of oppression rendered it especially ill-equipped to address the social polarisation which gripped the US during the Reagan-Bush years. This was a systemic phenomenon, which could only be misunderstood when forced into the confines of postmodern micro-analysis. Earnings growth slowed after 1973, while earnings inequality increased sharply after 1979.[16] The bottom 60 per cent of families experienced a drop in income between 1979 and 1991.[17] The average family income of the bottom 10 per cent fell by 12 per cent in the 1980s.[18] Income growth for black families – their median income already 40 per cent below that of white families – was slower during the period than that of white families. Family income of Hispanics actually declined during the 1979-89 period, causing the spread between white and Hispanic median family income to widen. Hispanic median income fell from 69.3 per cent of white median income in 1979 to 65.2 per cent in 1989. At the same time, the top 1 per cent of families saw spectacular income growth, so that by the end of the decade their income share matched that of the bottom 40 per cent.[19] These income trends were accompanied by the tremendous expansion of low-wage jobs and other forms of precarious employment. The percentage of US workers earning less than the poverty level for a family of four jumped from 12 per cent in 1979 to 18 per cent in 1992. For full-time workers between the ages of 18 and 24, the percentage working at the poverty level grew at an astounding pace – from 23 per cent in 1979 to 47 per cent in 1992. The largest amount of job growth took place in the lowest paying sectors: retail trade and services such as health.[20]

Postmodern theory was poorly situated to discuss these trends for two reasons. This body of theory was disabled by its culturalist bias.

First, these trends could scarcely be understood as constructions of a network of representations. They reflected such ugly, extra-textual realities as high interest rates, deindustrialisation and union-busting. At the same time, the trends were systemic and global in character. Because of its exclusive focus upon highly diverse and discontinuous local sites of oppression and resistance, postmodern social theory is unable to penetrate the reality of these trends.

Politically, the refusal to generalise or to develop a systemic critique of inequality, within which particular oppressions could be located, had a paradoxical effect. It made it much easier for discussions of particular oppressions to be outflanked and muffled by the bland references to the deteriorating situation of the 'middle class' during the 1980s, characteristic of the Clinton campaign. This theme was encapsulated in the motto, 'It's the economy, stupid!' This saying expressed a desire to marginalise discussion of particular oppressions which might be castigated by the Right as 'special interests'. The postmodernists' insistence on the discrete and singular character of the oppressions made them all the more vulnerable to such marginalisation. Without an attempt by the Left to situate special oppressions prominently within the overall trends towards social polarisation, Clinton-style avoidance of particular oppressions was made easier.

Of particular concern is the inherent inability of postmodern social theory to find a response to the sort of scapegoating argument presented in the Republican presidential campaigns of the 1980s. This position proceeds from general propositions about the interaction of the market, parliamentary democracy and interest groups to the racialised demonisation of 'special interests' in the Republican campaigns. It asserts the existence of powerful structural linkages between social instances, which work together to produce a particular exploitative outcome.

The inability of postmodern theory to confront neo-liberal social theory is, to a considerable degree, due to its culturalist emphasis. This theory focuses upon the formation of identities in particular milieus through networks of symbolic representation and power. As in the new social movements – the women's movement, the gay movement, the various movements against the oppression of particular ethnic groups – the focus in postmodern theory has been on oppression, not exploitation, as Ellen Meiksins-Wood has pointed out.[21] As she put it:

> The various struggles against oppression (as distinct from 'exploita-
> tion'?) which go under the name of the 'new social movements'
> derive their special character from a displacement of opposition
> away from capitalism, to other sets of oppressive relationships. In
> itself, the focus on targets often rendered invisible by traditional
> socialist preoccupations has enriched the socialist project. But much

has also been lost by the tendency to render capitalism itself invisible and to consider the conditions of human emancipation in abstraction from their determination by the dominant logic of capitalism. It is a very striking feature of the Western Left today that, across a wide spectrum, capitalism has apparently ceased to be the enemy.[22]

As anti-capitalism has waned on the Left, so has its ability to challenge open defenders of the capitalist order on their own ground. The failure of postmodernism in this regard is both a cause and consequence of the current peculiar state of affairs on the Left. In the face of sharpening inequality, the clear identification of the winners and losers helps both to develop a focused political agenda and prevent scapegoating. Any such scapegoating theory must be met on its own ground and challenged with a critique and a rival theory of exploitation. But such an alternative would have to present a historically-grounded theory of some generality concerning the obstacles to economic growth in recent decades, the current role of racism in US politics, the deepening of social inequality and the role of the Right and business interest groups in these developments. Without some such argument, and arguments of this type are simply beyond the range of postmodern theory, there is no way effectively to challenge the racially-charged scapegoat theory of the Right. A theory with an overwhelmingly culturalist focus cannot perform the necessary work.

By virtue of its scepticism, localism and culturalism, postmodern theory is inherently incapable of mounting any sort of effective attack on neo-liberal doctrine in its theoretical or practical forms. The assessment here is largely speculative, because no such attack has ever been tried, to my knowledge at least. One is finally inspired to ask how a doctrine so incapable of, and uninterested in, attacking capitalism and its defenders could attain such prominence on the Left? And how could it have attained such prominence in this period? Periods of sharpening social polarisation are ripe for a social theory which sets out from a theory of exploitation. Working people and the poor in such a period are bound to ask whether some other social group is benefiting from their worsening conditions of life. How has it come about that the concept of exploitation has been abandoned by the Left in just such a period and adopted by the Right, which uses it to sharpen divisions in the working class?

This development seems to reflect the long-term weakening of the Left, particularly the revolutionary Left, since the 1960s. Even in that decade, the bastions of revolutionary upsurge in Cuba and Vietnam found themselves quarantined by counter-revolutionary victories: the murderous defeat of Indonesian Communism in the east and the defeat of guerrilla movements in Latin America, capped by the disaster of successive coups or militarised rule in Uruguay, Chile and Argentina. In Europe, the far Left was largely coopted into resurgent social democratic parties, or chose to concentrate on changes in civil society via the new social movements. This predicament of defeat or withdrawal was accelerated by the conversion of regimes of the east to market principles: the rise of the pro-capitalist Deng faction in the Chinese Communist Party and the ascendancy of pro-western, business-oriented currents in the Soviet party. Such developments in the bureaucratised, post-capitalist regimes of China and Russia, their revolutionary days long since past, were of prime importance for ideological reasons and because they foretold the ending of material aid to revolutionary movements and liberation struggles. The complex, global rightward shift was, of course, capped by the final collapse of the Soviet Union. This wave of political defeats and the accompanying atmosphere of market triumphalism have encouraged an intellectual drift on the Left from questions of exploitation and class power towards often highly rarefied forms of cultural critique.[23]

With neo-liberals in the Kremlin and veterans of the Long March defending capitalism in China, we are a long way from the heady days of the Tet Offensive and the May Events. In this environment, postmodernism may be the path of least resistance for many Left intellectuals. One may sing the praises of resistance and contestation without committing oneself, even theoretically, to challenge the most heavily defended ideological positions of the Right on the virtues of the free market and the vices of the people and the state. With neo-liberalism promoting misery and inequality here at home, and economic disasters in Latin America, Africa and Russia, such evasions may become increasingly difficult to maintain.

References

1   F.A. Hayek, *Law, Legislation and Liberty*, vol.3, *The Political Order of a Free People* (Chicago, 1979), pp.22-35.
2   Ibid., p.99.
3   Ibid., pp.89-90.
4   Ibid., p.94.
5   Ibid., p.96.
6   Thomas Edsall and Mary Edsall, *Chain Reaction* (New York, 1991), p.206.
7   Ibid., pp.222-30.
8   See the arguments of the Federation for American Immigration Reform presented in William Hamilton, 'Harvest of blame', *Washington Post* (4 June 1993), 1A and 4A.
9   For an acute survey of leading theorists of the Right, including Hayek, which stresses their links to practical politics, see Perry Anderson, 'The intransigent Right', *London Review of Books* (Vol.14, no.18, 24 September 1992).
10   Mancur Olson, *The Rise and Decline of Nations* (New Haven, 1982). Worth special note is Olson's concept of 'jurisdictional integration' as a means of weakening interest groups, a discussion which seems particularly prescient with the expansion of NAFTA and the tightening of EC integration.

11 Ernesto Laclau and Chantal Mouffe, *Hegemony and Socialist Strategy* (London, 1985), p.111.
12 Ibid., pp.179-80.
13 Michel Foucault, *The History of Sexuality, Volume 1* (New York, 1978), p.7.
14 For an excellent short survey of the condition of the US poor at the end of the 1980s, see Elliott Currie, 'Heavy with human tears: free market policy, inequality and social provision in the United States', in Ian Taylor (ed.), *The Social Effects of Free Market Policies* (New York, 1990), pp.199-219.
15 Christopher Norris, who has persuasively criticised postmodern perspectivism in many works, gives a vivid demonstration of this proposition in *Uncritical Theory: postmodernism, intellectuals and the Gulf War* (Amherst, 1992).
16 Frank Levy and Richard Murnane, 'US earnings levels and earnings inequality: a review of recent trends and proposed explanations', *Journal of Economic Literature* (Vol. XXX, September 1992), pp.1333-81.
17 Lawrence Mishel and David Frankel, *The State of Working America 1992-1993* (Armonk, New York, 1993), p.13.
18 Paul Krugman, 'The income distribution disparity', *Challenge* (No.33, July/August 1990), p.4.
19 Mishel and Frankel, op.cit., pp.39, 49.
20 Jason DeParle, 'Sharp increase along the borders of poverty', *The New York Times* (31 March 1994), A-18; Mishel and Frankel, op.cit., p.173.
21 Ellen Meiksins-Wood, '"Civil society" and the devaluation of democracy', *Socialism in the World* (Nos 74-5, 1989), p.176.
22 Ibid., p.177.
23 For an elaboration of this argument see James Petras and Steve Vieux, 'The decline of revolutionary politics: capitalist detour and the return of socialism', *Journal of Contemporary Asia* (Vol.24, no.1, 1994).

LEE BRIDGES

Tory education: exclusion and the black child*

'There is no such thing as society. There are only individuals and families.'

Margaret Thatcher

Nowhere has the anti-social philosophy of Thatcherism been given greater rein than in the field of education. For the past five years, under its education 'reforms', the government has pursued a policy of fragmentation and atomisation of education, deliberately breaking down the social and political balance of the system that had been created and maintained under successive administrations and education acts from 1944 onwards. The aim has been to destroy this old system and to replace it with one giving precedence, under the slogans of 'choice' and 'diversity', to the most base instincts of individualism and familialism. In the process, potential points of organised resistance within the existing system – among local authorities, educational officials, teachers, governors, parents and pupils – to the openly ideological manipulation of education have been neutralised and destroyed.

This project can be compared with the other Thatcherite dream of destroying 'socialism' in eastern Europe, which in so many places has turned into the nightmare of inter-communal violence and ethnic cleansing. Educational reform in Britain has unleashed demons of its

Lee Bridges is a principal research fellow at the University of Warwick and research director at the Public Law Project. He was formerly a school governor and governor trainer.
* This is an expanded version of a chapter from *Outcast England: how schools exclude black children* by Jenny Bourne, Lee Bridges and Chris Searle (London, IRR, forthcoming).

Race & Class, 36, 1 (1994)

own. As schools are made, under the new market philosophy, to compete with one another – for money, for pupils, for reputation among parents stirred up to exercise 'choice' – then they, too, have begun to expel those who are seen as troublesome, too expensive, different. This includes the disabled, with their 'special needs', and, increasingly, black pupils who, because of their perceived 'behavioural problems', 'learning difficulties' or mere cultural differences, are seen as driving schools' examination results or attendance records down a notch on the 'league tables' and as being too costly or difficult to manage, let alone to educate.

From an education system to an education market

The 1944 Education Act had tried to mould a variety of different types of school into a single system, in particular by bringing together the previously separate state, church and charitably-endowed sectors of education under the umbrella of local education authorities. The system entailed a number of compromises and was built around a complex set of checks and balances, as between national government, local authorities and individual schools. National government would carry the main responsibility for funding education (even in church schools) through the system of general taxation and subsidies to local authorities, as well as providing overall supervision (but not direct control) of standards. It would also ensure the 'reasonable' behaviour of the other elements in the system towards each other. Schools themselves would retain a fair degree of autonomy over their internal organisation and practices. In the middle, local education authorities would have the main responsibility for determining educational policy in their areas and guaranteeing, through the provision of sufficient school places, the right to education for every child. The fulcrum of the system's checks and balances was, therefore, the concept of local democratic accountability as operated through the local education authority.

This system was not without its faults. It institutionalised both religious and class divisions, although in a somewhat muted form. Attempts by Labour governments in the 1960s and 1970s to eliminate such divisions, through a national policy of comprehensive education and a drive towards 'all ability' schools and teaching, foundered on the principles of local democratic control and individual school autonomy. Still, the system did guarantee a basic level of education for most of those in its charge and served as a vehicle of limited social mobility for the post-war generation of 'respectable' working-class children into the expanding bureaucratic and middle classes.

On the other hand, the system never came to terms with the aspirations of Britain's post-war black 'immigrants'. African-Caribbean children were labelled from the outset as 'under-achievers' and segregated within schools into lower 'streams' or teaching 'bands'. Subsequently, many African-Caribbean children were declared 'educationally sub-normal' and placed into special classes or separate schools on this basis. Asian children were equally segregated off by virtue of their language differences and local geography (via bussing). The system's failing of black children met with community – and not just parental – protest and resistance, which did not go without their successes. For example, the policy of separating out 'educationally sub-normal' pupils was eventually reversed in favour of their integration (under the rubric of 'educational special needs') into mainstream schooling. But such changes ended up, more often than not, in benefiting the white disadvantaged pupil more than black children in general.

The retreat from the principle of a single, universal system of education, catering equally for the needs of children of all backgrounds and abilities, began under the Labour government of the 1970s. The 'great debate' initiated by prime minister James Callaghan in October 1976 sought to shift the focus of education away from the child and his or her individual needs and more towards the demands of the economy:

> The goals of our education ... are to equip children to the best of their abilities for a lively, constructive place in society and also to fit them to do a job of work. Not one or the other, but both. For many years, the accent was simply on fitting the so-called inferior group of children with just enough learning to earn their living in the factory ... There is now a widespread recognition of the need to cater for the child's personality, to let it flower in the fullest possible way. The balance was wrong in the past. We have a responsibility now to see that we do not get it wrong in the other direction. There is no virtue in producing socially well-adjusted members of society who are unemployed because they do not have the skills.[1]

This new utilitarian emphasis in education has been traced to the economic crisis that confronted the Labour government following the OPEC oil price rises of the early 1970s.[2] But it also related directly to the social 'crisis' then becoming evident in Britain's inner cities around the position of 'second-generation' black youth. This group was seen as being neither economically nor socially 'well-adjusted'. On the one hand, they (and their parents) were considered to hold 'unrealistic aspirations' about the prospects of economic and social advancement in British society through education. On the other, they refused to accept their 'place' at the bottom of society or to show due deference to authority, especially as represented by the police. It was in order to address the symptoms of this problem within education that the Committee of Enquiry into the Education of Children from Ethnic Minority Groups was set up in July 1979. This was the body which (after a change of chairman from Anthony Rampton to Lord Swann) eventually produced the 1985 report, *Education for All*.[3] The report documented ethnic under-achievement in schools, especially among African-Caribbean boys, and attributed it to a variety of 'racial disadvantages' but primarily those rooted in black culture and family structure. In this, the Swann report echoed directly the Scarman report's portrayal of a 'culture of deprivation' in the African-Caribbean family, leading, among other social evils, to low achievement and behavioural problems at school.[4]

'Anti-racism' and educational 'reform'

By the time the Swann Committee reported, the Tories under Margaret Thatcher had been in power for six years. But, despite the clamouring of right-wing educational theorists dating back to the Black Papers in the late 1960s and early 1970s and Mrs Thatcher's own experience as secretary of state for education in the 1970-74 Heath government, little by way of major educational reform was attempted in the first two terms of the Thatcher regime. The major target of 'market reform' in this period was the economy and the trade unions, although education, like other locally-controlled social services, suffered from the general monetarist assault on public expenditure and local government finances in particular. However, as a portent of the future, the Education Act 1981 gave legal backing to 'parental choice' of schools for their children. Local authorities were only allowed to resist this on clear grounds of economy and efficiency in the overall provision of education in their areas. It was this parental right that white parents were subsequently to assert, most notoriously in Dewsbury,* in order to force local authorities to channel their children away from schools they regarded as having too many black pupils.

The period of the mid-1980s was also the high point of 'anti-racism' in education, sparked off by the protest of black youth in the urban rebellions and given some official legitimacy, at least in the Home Office if not the Department of Education and Science, by the Scarman and Swann reports. It was, after all, Home Office funds (fed through section 11 of the Local Government Act 1966) that provided the greater part of the finance for the London Borough of Brent's major programme of recruitment of 180 specialist teachers, as a means of counter-balancing the under-representation of black teachers in the borough and through this to attack the real problems of under-achievement among black

---

* In 1987, a group of white parents refused to send their children to the largely Asian school allocated to them by the local education authority (Kirklees), because the parents said they wanted their children to have an education based on 'British culture'. Supported by the Parental Alliance for Choice in Education, the case went to the High Court. In 1988, Kirklees education authority allowed the families to send their children to the schools of their own choice.

children. In the event, the programme was hijacked by the media and the Right, around the case of Maureen McGoldrick, as a vehicle for attacking not just 'anti-racism' and the so-called 'loony left' councils that had spawned it, but also the very idea of local, democratic accountability for education as a whole. At the same time, the Left, by the bureaucratic, 'top-down' manner in which it approached 'anti-racism', played directly into the hands of the Right:

> The fundamental error was to take up the 'anti-racism' package for want of properly thought-out policies tailored to local needs. Such a package had originally been cobbled together by Labour authorities (and especially the Greater London Council) as an institutional response to the 'riots' of 1981 and to Lord Scarman's discovery of 'racial disadvantage' and 'ethnic need'. Such 'anti-racism' made no distinction between individual racism and institutionalised racism, between personal power and institutional power, and opened the door to all kinds of 'skin politics' and white 'guilt tripping'. It was the adoption of such a slick package and the implementation of its ideas by officers that allowed the Council's fight over policies to appear as a vendetta against a few teachers. It was also why its fight ended up as a fight about the right to employ black teachers rather than as a fight for improving education for all children, in which black teachers were a means to an end.[5]

Certainly, there is little evidence that anti-racism enlisted the support of either teachers or black pupils, let alone the mass of black parents and the wider community. In part, this was because anti-racist policies became paper exercises, separated from the everyday life of schools and the struggles of committed forces within them to tackle the immediate need to improve the quality of education for all deprived pupils. To the less committed teachers, 'anti-racism' came to be perceived as little more than a bureaucratic policing exercise, forcing them for a time to suppress their more authoritarian tendencies and even racist sympathies, so that there was, most probably, a downturn in black exclusions from schools during this period, for fear of exposure through local authority 'monitoring'. But even this regulatory function of 'anti-racism' failed to build on the concept of black children's right to a decent education; it failed, that is, directly to assist them and their parents to fight for themselves the racism they encountered in schools over issues of 'streaming' and access to the curriculum, discipline and exclusions, and racial abuse and violence. Instead, as in the case of Ms McGoldrick, 'anti-racism' descended into

> a personalised fight against an individual – as though to change the person (or his or her personality) was to change the office, the institution. When such confusion is carried over into policy, it tends

not so much to alter the course of racial justice as to damage the larger fabric of natural justice. Ms McGoldrick ... was suspended ... on suspicion of being a racist (on the basis of a remark she is said to have made in a telephone conversation) and therefore in contravention of the anti-racist policies that the Council wished to carry out in education. At no point prior to suspension was she afforded a full hearing or accorded the benefit of her past record. And however much the issues might have been muddied by the yellow press or muddled by a reactionary teachers' union, the fact remains that the Council, in its anxiety to do right by black children, did wrong by Ms McGoldrick. Whereas, the fight for racial justice, if rightly fought, must of its very nature improve and enlarge justice for all.[6]

The history has not been written of how far the reactionary backlash over Ms McGoldrick (and the earlier media and union-backed outcry over the far less deserving case of another headteacher, Ray Honeyford, who came under criticism by black parents in Bradford) led the Tory Party finally to place educational reform at the centre of its electoral agenda in 1987. As noted, up to then the Thatcher government had not pressed legislative reforms in education, and the various Tory think-tanks had promoted a fairly disparate range of ideas. These included 'market-oriented' solutions, such as providing all parents with educational vouchers so as to allow them to 'purchase' places for their children at the schools of their choice (with unpopular schools thereby being left to wither away); the reintroduction of various forms of selection and specialism in secondary schools to counter the now dominant model of comprehensive education; the development of a 'national curriculum' to provide greater uniformity in the standards and content of state education; and a push towards a greater emphasis on science and technology in order to equip children for the rapidly changing employment market.

But it was just before the general election of 1987 that these various ideas were brought together around the central theme of the need to break the 'stranglehold' on education exercised by local authorities. In the process, the concept of local democratic accountability was to be replaced, on the one hand, by 'market accountability' of schools to parents and, on the other, by new national standards of education to be enforced by a burgeoning central government bureaucracy, backed by a plethora of politically-appointed advisory bodies covering, for example, every aspect of the curriculum.

Restructuring education

The process of breaking up the unified education system originally established under the Education Act 1944 began with the passage of the Education Reform Act 1988 and has continued apace under the subsequent Education Acts of 1992 and 1993. Building on the concept of 'parental choice' of schools, the 1988 Act removed local education authorities' residual powers to attempt to equalise the distribution of children across the schools in their areas. Local authorities would no longer be able to fix a maximum number of pupils to be admitted to a school below its physical capacity, nor were parents to be limited by factors of geography or even local authority boundaries in seeking school places for their children. It was also clear that this system of 'open enrolment' would primarily work to the advantage of middle-class parents, who would be in the best position to search out the 'good schools' and to meet the extra costs (eg, for travel) that might be required for their children to attend them. Although the government at the time was advised that such a system might readily be exploited by white parents in order to avoid schools with significant numbers of black pupils, thereby leading to racial segregation in education, it declared itself little concerned and was willing to let the 'market' of individual 'choice' in education predominate over any wider social values of racial integration and equality.[7]

Indeed, if local education authorities were to be stripped of their ability to seek to equalise the distribution of pupils, they were also to lose their powers to equalise or balance resources between schools according to the social and educational needs of different pupil groups. Up to the 1988 Act, both local education authorities and central government had employed various bureaucratic and financial mechanisms to channel additional resources to schools serving the most educationally and socially disadvantaged sectors of society. Funding formulae were geared in favour of areas with, for example, high proportions of pupils on free school meals or from single-parent families or ethnic minority backgrounds, as indicators of greater educational needs. But, under the 1988 Act, there was to be a shift towards 'delegated budgets', under which control over most public expenditure on education would pass from local education authorities, with their democratically-elected councils and education committees, into the hands of individual schools, nominally presided over by their governors. Most significantly of all, delegated budgets were to be determined strictly in line with a 'per capita' formula fixed on the number of pupils on each school's roll. All children, whatever their background of social and economic deprivation, were in future to be educated on a 'level playing field', so far as the availability of state funding was concerned. The 'per capita' funding formula also meant that schools would now compete with each other for finance through the 'market' of parental opinion and pupil recruitment.

Such a system of pupil-led 'market' competition between schools might have had two disadvantages for Tory reformers. It certainly fell short of the idea of educational vouchers, whereby parents would have been able to 'spend' their per pupil share of the public educational kitty outside the state system altogether, in the so-called 'independent' sector. Reformers had hoped through educational vouchers to stimulate the market for setting up new private and more selective schools, thereby leading all the more rapidly to the demise of the unified system of education built around local education authorities. A competitive 'market' operating between different schools all within the local education authority would be slow to redistribute children and resources in favour of the 'good schools' and, while limiting the power and influence of local authorities, would not lead to their destruction per se.

Under the 1988 Act, this problem was addressed by creating a system for existing state schools to 'opt out' of local authority control and to become grant-maintained schools, entirely 'self-governing' units but still wholly financed from public funds, now distributed directly to them by central government. In addition, a whole new class of secondary schools, with nominal private sponsorship and legally 'independent' in status, was to be created under the guise of city technology colleges (CTCs), even at the cost of tens of millions of pounds of additional state capital investment. And, if all schools that remained within the local authority sector were to be forced to compete on an equal financial footing, the government took steps (surreptitiously at first but later more openly) to rig the 'market' in favour of the grant-maintained schools and CTCs, by providing them with extra funding. Indeed, such funding was openly touted by ministers and their civil servants as a bribe for schools to exercise, through their parents and governors, their new 'right' to opt out of local authority control.

What was not so widely advertised was that the extra funding for grant-maintained schools and CTCs was to be deducted directly from the money available to the relevant local education authority to distribute to the rest of the schools within its area or from the centrally-controlled pool of capital funding from which all state schools had to bid for new buildings and improvements. In other words, having legislated to prevent local education authorities from redistributing funding between schools on the basis of pupils' social and educational needs, the government then imposed a redistributive formula of its own, geared to favour schools on grounds of their acceptability to – and acceptance of – market-led educational policy.

A second potential difficulty for Tory reformers was that shifting educational and financial control away from local education authorities and giving it to individual schools might open the way for greater parental and community influence over the content of education. While it might have been hoped by some Tory reformers that conservative sentiments among parents would thereby be given greater voice in schools, there could be no guarantee that other, more progressive forces in the community would not also seize the opportunity to restructure education in line with the needs of working-class and black children. (In a different context in the late 1960s and early 1970s, movements for 'community control of schools' were seen by black radicals in the United States as the only means of reforming urban education and combating the stifling, and often racist, influence of the educational bureaucracy and teachers' unions.) Some elements of the Tory educational Right did, in fact, embrace the idea of black business-sponsored CTCs or of Muslim schools to be supported through state funding (as with existing Anglican, Catholic and Jewish 'voluntary' schools), but specific proposals along these lines somehow always failed to reach fruition, or were ultimately rejected by the government.

More generally, the capacity for radical moves towards greater community influence over schools was to be stifled through new central controls over the curriculum and eventually through a system of more rigorous, 'independent' inspection, which gave the secretary of state draconian powers to take over any school adjudged to be 'failing'. The development of the national curriculum was assigned to centrally-controlled and politically-appointed advisory bodies, and it quickly evolved into a highly prescriptive, all-embracing set of guidelines which dictated how virtually every moment of the school day was to be filled and restricted the scope for teacher and/or pupil creativity in determining the content of their education. Inspections would, in turn, be geared to ensuring that schools stuck closely to the national curriculum and to measuring schools' performance through a set of standardised criteria, focusing in particular on examination results. Examinations, both in their content and in the way in which the results would be presented in 'league tables', left no space for differentiation as between individual children's needs. Rather, all children and schools, whatever the local social and economic context in which they developed or operated, were to be taught, tested and measured by the same simplistic standards.

In the process of this restructuring, the meaning of fundamental concepts has been transformed. Accountability has been stripped of its political and collective content, so that it no longer embraces the democratic expression of the community's need to provide a decent education for all its children, but is channelled instead through the much more narrow mechanism of individual 'choice' as operating in the educational market place. Schools are not only to be measured by simplistic 'league tables' that ignore their role in fulfilling the wider social needs of their pupils and communities, but 'league tables' are, in turn, to become the main means through which schools account for and advertise themselves (or, in the jargon, provide their 'consumers' with 'market information') and thereby compete with one another for pupils and money. Individual parents might be given the 'right' to complain if their child's school fails to adhere to the national curriculum, but parents collectively have no say in determining the content of that curriculum, or how it is applied in the teaching of their children.

The education 'reforms', by giving precedence to the opportunity of some parents to exercise 'choice', have also undermined the more fundamental right of each and every child to education. Certainly in law, the right to education has always been linked inextricably to the duty on local education authorities to secure a school place for every child in their area. Occasionally the legal force of this duty has been called into question, as when, in the dying days of the Inner London Education Authority, the courts failed to uphold an obligation on it to provide education for scores of Bangladeshi children in the London Borough of Tower Hamlets who had been denied school places.[8] But, so long as local education authorities held overall responsibility for the provision and financing of education, they were more usually able to fulfil their duty in the case of children left without school places, through processes of persuasion, convincing local schools to take them in without having to resort to formal legal sanctions. In the new situation where schools have 'opted out' of local authority control – or can threaten to do so, to the financial detriment both of the local education authority and other schools in the area – such informal processes of persuasion have broken down, and the legal powers of local authorities to require schools, even those nominally still within their control, to accept pupils have been exposed as weak and ineffectual. Children whose parents are unable, for whatever reasons, to play the new 'market' of school choice, or who are rejected by the system through non-admission or exclusion, find themselves cut adrift, with no effective means, formal or informal, of exercising their basic right to education.

The vicious circle of exclusion

It was inevitable that the Tory reforms would lead to an increase in pupil exclusions from school. Nor could it be expected that a government, which declared its indifference to the potential effects of 'open enrolment' in promoting racial segregation in schools, would give the least consideration to the likely impact of its policies at the other end of the process, in schools' practices of rejecting children through exclusions.

As the cases which we document elsewhere in this report show, exclusions are not caused by any single factor. Racism, both as reflected in the stereotypical assumptions and attitudes of individual teachers and governors towards black children and as institutionalised in policies that lead those children to be disproportionately identified as educationally backward or as presenting special behavioural problems, certainly plays its part in the processes leading to exclusion. But the problem of school exclusions is by no means limited to black children, or even to deprived urban areas. Equally, the recent sharp rise in exclusions can be traced to intensifying pressures at several different points – in the child's family and social setting, in schools among teachers and governors, and among local education officials and support services.

Black families have come under growing social and economic pressures as a direct result of government policies, trapped as they so often are in the most deprived and neglected inner urban areas and concentrated among the lower income sectors of society. For it is these sectors which have suffered most from rising unemployment, regressive taxation and massive cutbacks in social spending, not least in subsidies for public housing. Black parents and children alike also face the additional disruption to their lives resulting from rising racial harassment and attacks. All these factors combine to increase the discontinuity faced by many black children as between the social dislocation imposed on their family and community life and the demands of the supposedly more 'disciplined' and orderly school environment. It is hardly surprising that some black children present themselves as 'aggressive' in school, as this is a stance that society outside has taught them is necessary for survival. And, when racism spills over into the school itself, in terms of incidents or violence in the playground or in teachers' attitudes towards black pupils, black pupils are only confirmed in their aggression as a means of survival.

Teachers, in turn, have come under increased pressures due to the bureaucratic demands of the national curriculum and its associated paperwork, all of which leaves then with reduced time and often even fewer reserves of patience to deal sympathetically with the disruptive child in their midst. As a result, there is more frequent resort to in-school disciplinary measures – 'sending them to the duty room' – that enable classroom teachers to dispense quickly with difficult children and to 'get on with the real job' of 'delivering the curriculum'. In many schools, these measures have become a form of internal exclusion, cutting the children subject to them off from normal processes of education and school life. And such penalties quickly escalate into a series of 'fixed term' exclusions, until eventually their accumulated weight or some single major incident 'requires' the child, in line with a system of progressively more severe punishments, to be 'indefinitely' or 'permanently' excluded. It is often only at this stage that the school's governors and the local education authority are apprised of the child's disciplinary record, by which time the scope for more constructive intervention, in the form of support teaching or educational psychological or social counselling services, will have been overtaken by events. In any event, recommendations for such measures are likely to be perceived by the headteacher and staff of the school as a direct challenge to their authority and disciplinary decisions.

The opportunities for alternative solutions are also being constantly curtailed as the local education authority's share of the 'aggregate school budget' is gradually reduced in favour of greater financial delegation to schools. Frequently, it is support services such as educational psychologists and social workers which are the first to be cut back in this process. And, as local education officials find that their own resources and authority are eroded, they are less likely to seek to challenge individual headteachers or school governors over exclusions.

The whole system of 'checks and balances' built into the formal procedures for reviewing and appealing against exclusions has been undermined. The role of headteachers (who retain the sole power to exclude pupils from schools) has been transformed increasingly into that of 'managers' rather than 'educators', making them all the more conscious of the budgetary and other consequences of retaining difficult or disruptive children on their rolls. Governors are also required to bear greater responsibilities, not only for school budgets, but also for personnel relations and teacher retention, and are therefore reluctant to take any action that will alienate them from their headteacher and staff. In this situation, it is increasingly unrealistic to expect governors to exercise independent oversight over headteachers' decisions to exclude or to provide a forum for a fair and impartial hearing of parental and pupil appeals.

So, in the absence of intervention from the local education authority (which does not apply in the case of 'opted out' schools) parents wishing to challenge their child's exclusion are left only with an appeal to an 'independent' panel set up by the local authority or by the governors of the 'opted out' school. By this stage, the child may already have been out of school for several months while the parents, usually with no local sources of help or advice, have struggled through the earlier stages of review and, in the process, may have themselves been subject to questioning as to the conditions of their own family life and their 'failure' to support the school in its attempts to 'reform' the child. Little wonder that the statistics show that only in a tiny minority of exclusions do parents persist and fight through to the final stage of 'independent' appeal – but rarely with much success.[9]

All the elements in the new education market are therefore caught in a vicious circle, a cycle that leads inexorably towards the exclusion of increasing numbers of children from school and to the effective denial of their right to education. Nor is it just the growing incidence of exclusions, or their disproportionate impact on black children, that is so worrying. It is particularly disturbing to find that exclusions, especially against African-Caribbean boys, are being more frequently resorted to by primary and junior schools. It seems remarkable that in a modern society such measures of institutionalised punishment and official stigmatisation of young children can be regarded as an appropriate response to their social and behavioural problems. At the other end of the scale, there appears to be a tendency for older children, in their final year before leaving secondary school, to be excluded even for such minor 'disciplinary' infringements as failing to wear proper school uniform or to have appropriate haircuts. In these circumstances, there is an obvious link between the use of the sanction of exclusion and the school's desire to protect its reputation as reflected in examination 'league tables'.

Abrogating responsibility

Belatedly, the government has woken up to the fact of the growing numbers of children being excluded from school, if not to the origins of the problem in its own reforms.[10] The government's current concern over exclusions may owe a good deal to their effect in releasing 'anti-social' children into the community where they may 'drift into crime'.

In the past year, the government has moved in quick succession from a discussion paper on exclusion, through limited legislative reforms in the Education Act 1993, to the issuing, in a wave of publicity, of a set of draft circulars containing a mass of advice to schools and local education authorities on pupil behaviour and exclusions.[11] Separately, the new 'independent' schools inspectorate, the Office for Standards in Education (Ofsted), has issued reports on education for disaffected pupils[12] and on achieving good behaviour within schools.[13] These various documents go to considerable lengths to highlight the issue of growing numbers of children being excluded from school, including the disproportionate effect of exclusions on black children, and recounting the numerous poor practices and attitudes which contribute to the problem. Yet, there is a marked reluctance on the part of the government to move beyond strictures and exhortation in order to take effective action to curb the powers of schools to exclude pupils or, even more importantly, to redress the political imbalance and moral vacuum their market reforms have created in the education system at local level.

Apart from eliminating the anomaly by which schools can currently retain their budget share relating to an excluded pupil for the remainder of the school year in which the exclusion takes place, the government has limited its legal changes under the 1993 Act to the following. It has abolished the category of 'indefinite exclusions' (but replaced them with the opportunity to exclude pupils for longer 'fixed terms'); brought in new procedures whereby local education authorities or the new funding agency for grant-maintained schools will have the legal power to direct alternative schools (but not CTCs) to admit excluded pupils on to their rolls, and introduced a new duty on local education authorities to provide education to excluded pupils 'otherwise than at school'. Headteachers will now be empowered to exclude pupils on a 'fixed term' basis for up to fifteen days in each school term. There is a danger that headteachers may seek to use a series of extended 'fixed term' exclusions (which can amount in total to a quarter of the school year) as a means of circumventing the closer scrutiny of their decisions that would result from permanent exclusions and in order to keep difficult children out of school for long periods and thereby 'persuade' parents to remove them 'voluntarily' from the school. The government's recently issued draft circular on exclusions recognises the existence of such 'voluntary exclusions' and their effects in by-passing the legal safeguards designed to protect pupils and their parents, but it does no more than express disapproval of the practice.[14]

Indeed, none of its enlightened advice and guidance is backed up with new legal or administrative controls over schools, or rights for pupils and parents. Instead, the draft circular merely intends a tightening up of the time limits under which the current complex and inadequate procedures for reviewing and appealing against exclusions are carried out. In the absence of more fundamental reforms to simplify the procedures, provide a stronger independent check over all decisions to exclude permanently, and ensure that parents have readily accessible sources of advice and support in exercising their rights of appeal, all the draft circular is likely to achieve is to speed up the processes through which more and more children are being ejected from schools up and down the country.

Nor is the new legal power contained in the 1993 Act, for local education authorities to direct alternative schools to accept excluded pupils on to their rolls, likely to prove very effective. The power itself can only be used once the parents have approached and had their child rejected by every suitable school within the locality, and even then the school subject to such a direction (but not the pupil or parents) will have a right to appeal against it to the secretary of state. In this, the new proviso confirms the government's bias to protect the right of at least some schools to reject pupils that may harm their reputation rather than that of the children to have ready access to education.

The government's intentions in this area are, perhaps, encapsulated in the new legal responsibility placed on local education authorities to provide education for excluded pupils 'otherwise than at school'. In practice, this is likely to mean that local education authorities will find themselves, under pressure from increased school exclusions, having to set up and/or provide more places for such children at what are now called 'pupil referral units'. The Ofsted report on education for disaffected pupils was highly critical of the 'education' provided in many such units, which is often confined to only a few hours' tuition a week for each pupil in a very limited range of subjects and which, for older pupils, often amounts to little more than a containment operation until they reach minimum school-leaving age.[15]

Again, the government has now responded to these criticisms by issuing a draft circular exhorting local education authorities to provide better facilities and a fuller curriculum within 'pupil referral units'.[16] But the circular fails to address the crucial problem of resources or of the rights of parents and pupils in relation either to the education available in such units or to early readmittance to mainstream schooling. 'Pupil referral units' will not, for example, have governing bodies with parental or community representation, nor has the government stipulated even a minimum number of hours per week during which children in such units should receive education. And, while the draft circular proposes that a child's placement in a 'pupil referral unit' should be reviewed at least once a term, it is not proposed that this be made a legal requirement, enforceable by parents.

Without more effective controls and stronger rights for parents and pupils, both to prevent exclusions from taking place in the first instance and to ensure that excluded pupils receive their full rights to education and can be readily reintegrated into alternative mainstream schools, there is a real danger that 'pupil referral units' will become the 'educationally sub-normal schools' of the 1990s. And, with the growing evidence that it is black children who are most likely to be subject to exclusion and to rejection when their parents attempt to find alternative schools for them, we may again face the prospect of growing black community protest and disaffection from the education system as a whole.

References

1 Speech by prime minister James Callaghan at Ruskin College, Oxford (22 October 1976), quoted in Clyde Chitty, 'From Great Debate to Great Reform Act' in A. Rattansi and D. Reeder (eds), *Rethinking Radical Education* (London, 1992), p.31.
2 Ibid, pp.30-31.
3 The Swann Report, *Education for All* (London, 1985).
4 The Scarman Report, *The Brixton Disorders, 10-12 April 1981* (London, 1981).
5 A. Sivanandan, 'Race, class and Brent' in *Communities of Resistance: Writings on Black Struggles for Socialism* (London, 1990), p.142.
6 A. Sivanandan, 'Left, Right and Burnage' in ibid, p.146.
7 See remarks by Kenneth Baker, then secretary of state for education, on the Jimmy Young programme (BBC Radio 2), quoted in the *Times* (10 September 1987) and by Baroness Hooper, under-secretary for education, on television, quoted in the *Independent* (15 January 1988), to the effect that racial segregation of schools might well be a consequence of parental choice.
8 *R v Inner London Education Authority, ex p. Ali and Murshid, Times* (21 February 1990).

9 See Department for Education Discussion Paper, *Exclusions* (London, 1992).
10 Ibid.
11 Department for Education, *'Pupils with Problems' Draft Circulars* (London, December 1993).
12 Office for Standards in Education, *Education for Disaffected Pupils* (London, 1993).
13 Office for Standards in Education, *Achieving Good Behaviour in Schools* (London, 1993).
14 *'Pupils with Problems' Draft Circular No 3, Exclusion from School*, para.35.
15 Ibid, paras 14-31.
16 *'Pupils with Problems' Draft Circular No 4, Education by LEAs of Children Otherwise than at School.*

IAN MUNT

Eco-tourism or ego-tourism?

In recent years, the Third World has steadily emerged from the exclusive images of cataclysmic crisis – of starvation, deprivation and war – to represent the opportunity for an exciting, 'out-of-the-way' holiday. Praised for their environmental beauty and ecological diversity, travel to many Third World countries has been promoted by the new middle classes as a means of preserving fragile ecological landscapes and providing an 'ethnically' enhancing encounter. At the same time, some Third World governments have seized upon this new-found interest and promoted tourism as an opportunity to earn much-needed foreign exchange, as a last-ditch attempt to break from the confines of underdevelopment and get the IMF to lay the golden egg of an upwardly-mobile GNP.

Because the tourism debate has been too often couched in terms of the economic or environmental contribution it is able to make to Third World societies, the complexities of class and race have been largely neglected. In particular, the spectre of neocolonialism, which engenders a subtle but pervasive racism, has remained hidden. What, then, are the dimensions of these new tourisms, how do they embody class relations and why do they remain problematical?

With the notable changes in the advanced capitalist economies, there has been an attendant shift away from the traditional mass-packaged holidays, typically described as the 'sun, sea, sand and sex' experience, to the 'Ts' of the new tourism (travelling, trekking and trucking) that fit within the exciting and adventurous lifestyles of the new middle classes. These flexibly packaged, individually oriented

Ian Munt teaches geography at the University of the South Bank, London.

Race & Class 36, 1 (1994)

tourisms are now of increasing significance, catering for a more 'authentic' experience and characteristically claiming environmental and cultural sensitivity. Of these tourism practices, which range from archaeo-tourism to anthro-tourism, it is undoubtedly ecologically and environmentally founded travel that has attracted the greatest attention – the US-based Eco-tourism Society (established in 1990) refers to an 'Ecotourism Revolution'. While mass tourism has attracted trenchant criticism as a shallow and degrading experience for Third World host nations and peoples, new tourism practices have been viewed benevolently and few critiques have emerged. In particular, little has been said about the role of the new middle classes in the new social movements that have arisen, especially around the notion of 'other' cultures and the environment and ecological issues. Exactly who are these bearers of new moral values and how are their lifestyles reflected in travel?

'Having a fine time: glad you're not here'

This is how the taste-maker of the new middle-class attitudes, the *Independent*, describes the growth of what it calls the 'Snob Holiday-maker'. It cites the trips of John Cleese, Mick Jagger and Koo Stark to the hard-to-visit Himalayan kingdom of Bhutan as the summit of such practices.[1] Or, as it has advocated elsewhere, 'Out goes the "'ere we go" Costa-style tourism, in comes a more thoughtful middle-class approach'.[2] Holidays have become important commodities through which the new middle classes are able to proclaim their worldly status. Thomson Holidays' 'Travel à la Carte' holiday brochure urges you to 'choose from the menu or dream up a dish of your own'. Barrett refers to 'delicatessen' travel agents.[3] For the delicate, discriminating and generally luxurious, these offer holidays to 'an off-the-beaten-track, out of the way place'.[4] As Africa Exclusive, a tour company specialising in East African safaris, put it: 'gastronomy is taken as seriously as zoology'. Or, as an article in the *Observer* blurts, 'ECO-TOURISM ... It's not in any dictionary yet, but if you want to impress at your next dinner party, it's a dead cert.'[5] These are tourists who appear to conform to the journalistic image: *eco*-tourists, older and professionally successful, the 'cream of Manhattan and the City'.[6]

There are also the financially less well-endowed or the 'emergent urban-based, alienated petit bourgeoisie', in Gordon's description of tourists in Namibia, who became more 'tasteful' and mindful of environmental issues during the 1980s.[7] This is a tourism more characteristic of less formalised forms of travel, such as backpacking (and including tertiary-level students), often involving longer holidays overseas, especially in Third World regions. These are the *ego*-tourists, searching for a style of travel reflective of an 'alternative' lifestyle.[8] But, at the end of the day, the boundaries between these new middle-class fractions are blurred and they are united both by their ability to make relatively expensive journeys overseas and by seeking a classificatory distinction from run of the mill tourists.

Beyond stoking up on cultural capital, new tourisms have begun to be conceived (especially among the new petit bourgeoisie) as reflecting personal qualities in the individual, such as strength of character, adaptability, sensitivity or even 'worldliness'. Travel has become an increasingly professionalised appendage of the new middle-class lifestyle – a Victorianesque tour that enhances cultural appreciation and which is saturated with the inverted racism and patronisation characteristic of earlier travel habits.

A simple listing of adjectives prefixed to the traveller gives some clue to the qualities embodied in this hybrid tourist: adventurous, broad-minded, discerning, energetic, experienced, keen, imaginative, independent, intrepid, 'modern', real and true. But, if these qualities are insufficient, there are other prerequisites which help define such travellers. High Place's tours of India, for example, demand 'patience, stamina, humour and adaptability', and Journey Latin America cite 'essential qualifications for all trips' as 'emotional balance, maturity, a spirit of adventure and a desire for good companionship'.

Indeed, for tour operators catering more for the young and adventurous traveller, it is the invidious distinction between participant travellers and tourists that is of the essence. This is particularly notable among 'overlanding' operators such as Dragoman, which specialises in taking truck-loads of young, adventurous travellers into the 'wilderness', a world 'shunned by the masses who prefer the resorts and beaches'. Or, as Explore puts it in its brochures, travel for 'people who want more out of their holiday than buckets of cheap wine and a suntan'.

What effect, though, are these largely white, middle-class, right-on, latter-day missionaries (or wayfarers!) having as they fan out across the Third World regions of the globe? What do these new tourism practices mean and what are they a part of? I would suggest there are three indelible birth-marks of the new tourism.

Intervention and commodification

The spread of capitalist relations of production and widespread commodification throughout the Third World is one of the most notable global processes of the post-1960s era. International tourism has been an important conduit of this process. As Truong notes in her study of South East Asia, 'there has been a high degree of external influence on the formation of tourism and leisure policies', a pressure exerted by foreign governments, global financial institutions such as the World Bank and by development agencies.[9] But the pressure and external meddling have now changed course, away from the enthusiastic support for mass tourism, to new, 'softer' forms of tourism that augur well for the sustainability discourse of postmodernisation; a discourse adopted and promoted by the 'international community', capitalist business and the new social movements mobilised around ecology that are now commonplace in the west. Environmentalism is the sounding-board for these conflicting interests and sustainability has itself emerged as a precept of ideological proportions. And, within this context, tourism is being upheld as both the cause and effect of environmental and, to a lesser extent, cultural preservation.

Through a range of initiatives, from the 'debt-for-nature' swaps pioneered by the US government,[10] to lending agencies placing environmental conditions and caveats on their loans and grants, to the phenomenal growth in 'green tourist' operators, a *greening* of social relations is promoted, an eco-structural adjustment. The Domestic Technology Institute (DTI), a US-based, non-profit organisation, is currently planning a 'multinational organisation to develop and co-ordinate low-impact tourism in Third World countries'. As DTI spokesperson Lillywhite boasted, Third World countries 'can be forced into establishing a natural and cultural resource policy before they can get World Bank loans'.[11]

Through the economics of bio-diversity, a concept adopted by organisations such as the World Wildlife Fund, the International Union for Conservation of Nature and Conservation International (part of whose efforts seek to link up Third World communities with US corporate buyers), global groups are able to meddle in Third World affairs. At their most powerful, donor agencies and environmental organisations join forces to pursue conservation policies in which tourism is a major economic factor. As Gordon demonstrates in the case of Namibia: 'Adjusting the sales of tourism, Nature Conservation began to explore the viability of elite expeditions to "natural and wild" parts.'[12]

Other interventionist methods have also emerged among environmental organisations and are being successfully employed, as when, for example, the multinational Programme for Belize began to sell certificated acres of Belizean forest in an operation that was the antithesis of local control. As their UK newsletter says:

> Buy an acre for a loved one, or for yourself ... the best way of spreading the word is to buy those near and dear to you an acre for themselves. Nearly half the donations we receive are made as gifts on behalf of partners, friends and family and we particularly enjoy sending off packages as christening gifts, wedding presents, anniversary celebrations, etc. We know from the response that, whatever the occasion, it is the perfect present.[13]

Similar schemes are run by other organisations, such as Conservation International. Another ingenious approach, adopted by an increasing number of independent tour operators, is to become actively involved in the management of private conservation areas in the ultimate attempt to protect their principal commodity. For example, World-wide Journey and Expeditions, in its 1992 brochure, claims manage-ment involvement in the only 'privately' managed national park in Africa, Kasanka (Zambia).

At this level, it is the 'pristine environment' and 'wildlife' that form the principal commodities. Socio-cultural considerations of class and race are marginalised, non-existent. The problematic has been to formulate economic models which can be used to assign monetary value to wildlife and activities such as wildlife viewing but have yet to be advanced to native peoples.

For the individual representatives of this new tourist middle-class, it is their desire to confirm and legitimate their cultural and environmen-tal sensibilities that is inherent in their concern with ecology and Third and Fourth World 'otherness'. Encounter Overland, an overland trucking company, explains the 'adventure traveller' as 'today's custo-dian of the ancient relationship between traveller and the native which throughout the world has been the historic basis for peaceful contact'.

The basis of this new tourism is the discovery of 'lesser-visited', 'off-the-beaten-track', or 'even further off the beaten track' areas (Asian Affairs tour company), that either 'receive very few tourists' (Detours, 92) or are 'tourist free'. There are even whole countries that are for the 'traveller rather than the tourist', as Meon, a tour operator, describes Ecuador. Take this article in Trailfinders' travel brochure, for example, dealing with trekking in northern Thailand: 'As the popularity of this type of holiday experience increases it is more difficult to find ... untouched or traditional villages.' Trailfinders offers treks to villages 'which are only visited a couple of times a month. These groups are welcomed as a refreshing diversion to normal village life.' The brochure underscores a nostalgic desire for the imagined, 'real' and 'authentic' primitiveness, and itself calls for cultural preservation, in a new twist to the institutionalisation of racism.

It is the colonial emphasis on discovery and expropriation that has been rediscovered within a neo-colonial tourism. Latin America, in travel discourse, is the 'ultimate frontier' (Journey Latin America), while for tours to Africa, Dr Livingstone is frequently invoked to assist in hedonistic discoveries. For example, J & C Voyageurs promises of Malawi: 'Following in the footsteps of Dr Livingstone, gliding quietly up the Shire River, unchanged since the first appearance of the white man.' Or let Africa Exclusive, another tour operator, express its thoughts on Zimbabwe: 'When we first discovered this beautiful country – like the great missionary and explorer Dr David Livingstone

150 years earlier – we were very excited.' Forms of colonial travel and holidaying have also re-emerged into popularity, with luxury safaris widely offered, such as the 'Classic Kenya' described by Worldwide Journeys and Expeditions as 'an escorted private safari in the old style tradition' in a 'series of luxuriously appointed mobile tented camps'.

This is romanticism for both the wildness and travel modes of the colonial period, in which racism and class subordination are recreated in more invidious forms. Racism is not only institutionalised, but commodified as well. And it has invoked a nostalgic longing for untouched, *primitive* and native peoples.

Subjugation, subservience and servility

Jost Krippendorf argues that tourism will remain 'a special form of subservience', unless the industry and practice of tourism undergoes a dramatic and profound restructuring.[14] It is nothing short of arguing that the widely cited 'Ss' of tourism – sun, sea and sand – are matched by the 'Ss' of the content and outcome of tourism – subjugation, subservience and servitude.

It is obvious, as the political economy of tourism demonstrated, that Third World countries especially are subordinated to the touristic currents that flow from and to the advanced capitalist economies.[15] Analysing tourism from such an approach should not, however, limit comment to the huge multinational tour companies or to the effect of external factors, such as war or terrorism, on Third World holiday destinations. It should embrace the holiday consumption practices and preferences of the new middle classes. In addition, it should seek to understand the processes external to many Third World countries where the industry has produced a helpful, smiling and servile tourism class, serving the interests and economic preferences of business and political elites. Even after training courses and 'tourism weeks', Jean Holder (the jet-setting secretary general of the Caribbean Tourism Organisation) complains:

> aggressive attitudes ... often emerge [which] have their basis, to some extent, in the fact that a significant number of employees are not proud of what they do, and harbour resentments rooted in the inability to distinguish between service and servitude.[16]

More likely, however, and despite the arrival of the new eco-ethnic tourists, is the continuance, within the structures of the tourist industry, of the deeply embedded racial and class-bound institutionalised discriminatory processes which, on a larger scale, have proved so successful in promoting Caribbean states from a condition of colonial dependence into highly stratified reflections of their former colonial masters. It should, perhaps, be no surprise that political and business elites in such a set-up are unable to comprehend the feelings engendered within the tourism workforce. Whereas, within industrial capitalism, labour has to confront its subordination in the industrial hierarchy, within tourism, labour in many cases has also to confront the personification of its servility, the tourist, daily. The tourist product is embodied within the interactions and social relations that tourist and worker experience. At one level, then, the central property of commodities of which Marx speaks so convincingly – the fetishistic 'mist' that enshrouds, masks and objectifies labour – dramatically clears within much tourism as the guest is faced with the servant.

For the new tourism to claim that servility and subordination are overcome is highly disingenuous. The number of tourists involved and whether they are packaged in a conventional sense is secondary. I have already noted the neo-colonial aura that is recreated through eco-safaris, for example. This is symbolically reproduced by J & C Voyageurs. In the single black and white photograph offered in its brochure (all other photographs are large colour photographs of wildlife), a trail of porters (thirty-five, they tell us) are shown tramping through an eco-colonial landscape, carrying the supplies for the group of six, 'most of the comforts of home – iced drinks, spacious sleeping tents, loos and showers'. It is an image and ambience that is recreated by many new, independent tour operators, whether it be luxury safaris or treks and expeditions for the young and adventurous; an army of global porters trot behind or ahead (via different routes) to ensure that these new ethical tourists are regularly refreshed.

But it is through gender that subordination finds its marriage with race and class consummated. Sex-tourism has emerged as a major activity especially associated with the 'orientalism' of Asia.[17] As Edward Said depressingly catalogues in demonstrating this 'formidable structure of cultural domination', orientalism represents such a 'system of truths' that it has 'rarely offered the individual anything but imperialism, racism and ethnocentrism for dealing with "other" cultures'.[18] The most persistent 'good' of western cultural life is sex: sexual experimentation and fantasy, promise, desire, delight and unlimited sensuality. It is this key feature of orientalism (carefully nurtured by the nineteenth century's colonial wayfarers) that has been so cleverly refined in the 'postmodern' world of mass communications, while remaining the standardised cultural stereotype that is 'the mysterious Orient', smiling, servile and sexy. The Orient has emerged as a 'mythic language' in which such values are recreated time and again in, perhaps, the ultimate process of subordination as embodied in the burgeoning brothel culture of the sex-tourism industry.

In an attempt to persuade the jury to conclude the innocence of tourism, Kutay (a tour operator and director of the US Ecotourism Society) crassly stumbles upon the critical question: 'Those who view tourism as the final, most humiliating stage of human domination condemn it ... But is modern tourism any more dominating or humiliating than religious imperialism or European mercantilism?'[19] Indeed, it is not, but it can be analysed as on a par with those phenomena: tourism remains a highly interventionist and subordinating industry. It is the last of its key characteristics, fetishism, that seals its fate.

Fetishism and aestheticisation

Even when the mist that obscures social and labour relations in tourism momentarily clears, what remains is still blurred and mutated, for tourism is a highly-charged, fetishistic practice. It is an avenue through which our 'world-views' are shaped and then concretised through the vortex of our multi-media experiences – travel reviews, travel programmes and documentaries, travel brochures and guides, advertising and popular experience and exchange. If there is one advance or success that we might have expected new, more 'aware' tourism practices to achieve, it would have been to clarify and expose this level of fetishism. By contrast, the alternative travel lobby has provided the foundation for new, more ingenious and intellectualised ways through which class practice and racism are institutionalised.

The veteran war correspondent, Martha Gellhorn, writing in the *Independent on Sunday*, is one exemplar of the buffoonery of other 'travel writers'. For Belize, the former colony of British Honduras, and now a much desired ecological destination favoured by eco-tourists, is simply deemed 'too good for tourists'. Her exposition is reminiscent of bygone travelogues: 'Untainted by tourism, Belizeans are lovely.' It is an unsophisticated, race-oriented ethnography that Gellhorn offers – ranging from her observation of Mayan 'Spanish speaking bird-like women, all married at 14, all giggly and happy with hordes of children', to the Garifuna, 'matt black, with sharp strong Indian features, and a reserved ungiggly manner'. But she also celebrates the 'achievements' of colonialism: 'These self-confident people are loyal subjects of the Queen ... they don't know how lucky they are, past and present.'

It is in the stream of touristic images that fetishism is most visibly maintained. Out, or at least marginalised, are the images of long, sandy, palm-fringed beaches. In are the images of unlimited wildlife, adventure landscapes and painted indigenous cultures. In many of the brochures representative of the new tour operators, wildlife and natives are synonymous. Passive, they are to be discovered, sighted, viewed and, ultimately, 'shot'. In fact, the treatment of animals and peoples has become dramatically inverted within a neo-colonial context, allowing Cara Spencer Safaris to promise of South Africa: 'A bonus for us was the warmth, concern and courtesy of the people ... And their approach to wildlife conservational land management is highly progressive.'

Behind the images, which, like wildlife, are carefully preserved, life is infinitely more complex, for, as James Painter argues of a popular postcard in Guatemala depicting women coffee pickers dressed in the brilliantly coloured indigenous costumes adored by travellers, 'it would be hard to imagine a more distorted image of reality'.[21] Racism is not only institutionalised and commodified, but it is reproduced and fashioned through the media, so that we increasingly consume false images of what we are supposed to value, whether of the native hill tribes of northern Thailand or Mayan Indians in Guatemala. We are no longer able to transcend or look beyond the 'smiling faces', or challenge this image-reality. As Krippendorf argues, it is not that people do not, or cannot, 'see through the clichés', but that they are complicit in being 'seduced by them, again and again'.[22]

The liberal, new middle classes have, then, learnt how to celebrate difference, diversity and 'otherness' and aestheticise its reality. Tucan, a company specialising in adventure tours to South America 'to meet the needs of younger travellers', encapsulates the 'real' Latin America experience:

> Enormously wealthy people in their impressive mansions and estates live virtually cheek by jowl with the very poor in their squalid adobe huts and yet the populace as a whole show a special friendliness coupled with a real sense of hospitality.

Widescale repression of human rights, deeply rooted racism and intense class political struggle are null and void in the brave new world of adventure travel.

It is necessary only to think of the stream of tours to, for example, Kenya, Thailand or, of course, the former apogee of racism, South Africa, to imagine and predict the fetishistic effect that is the order of new tourism. And it is not only the luxury tours and safaris (mentioned above), offered by the new independent tour operators, that mask reality. Take backpacking, for example, supposedly the earthiest of alternative travel modes. Here is what the travel guide, *Backpacker's Africa*, had to say of Kenya: 'blessed with outstanding geographical and cultural variety ... her relatively stable government and capitalist economy is an added attraction for visitors'.[23]

Among the younger, new petit-bourgeois travellers, it is the authentication of their anticipated experiences that is of the cultural essence; they are unwilling to accept the reality of change and are sceptical about authenticity. So, as Trailfinders warns in outlining 'changes to the authentic traditional village' in the north of Thailand, 'be prepared for ... more foreigners than [you] had hoped to see, traditional costume frequently forsaken in favour of modern clothing, imported artifacts for sale and eating in separately-built visitors' accommodation'.

In the more problematic and 'unsavoury' situations with which travellers are confronted (supposedly not cushioned by the tourist comforts of yesteryear's industry), reality can be fetishised and marginalised in other ways. A company such as Tours to Remember contrasts its tours to what it calls the eastern equivalent of Benidorm in which 'mass travel [is] marketed like beans'. Concerning India, for example, the managing director professes, 'I do not claim to understand India, only to enjoy and respect its many virtues and hope that less attractive aspects will eventually disappear' ('India and Beyond'). Gross poverty, powerlessness and structures saturated in discriminatory processes are simply irritants in this approach.

By contrast, what I term 'aestheticisation' incorporates, integrates and embraces the brutal reality, rather than stepping aside from it. That reality is then glorified and becomes intrinsic to the uniqueness and quality of *adventure* travel, a bitter twist for those young adventure travellers visiting unstable regions such as Central America, who can now include army checkpoints, state repression and civil strife on their list of things to tick off.[24]

Reading like the script to Oliver Stone's *Salvador*, another travel article, entitled 'Weekending in El Salvador', begins to express the sickly aestheticisation that stimulates these middle-class leeches, experiences from which they are able to suck:

> the tension-filled journey to El Salvador was not one that we wished to prolong ... Apprehensiveness hung in the air like smoke ... Five hours later we arrived at the Salvadorean border ... We had been careful not to bring in anything remotely *subversivo* – Graham Greene, Joan Didion and Patrick Marnham left reluctantly behind. ... Finally satisfied that we weren't revolutionaries or agents of the left Farabundo Marti Front for National Liberation, they let us through ... we started to count all the men in round helmets and pale green uniforms ... Everywhere we looked there they were: American M16 machine guns slung casually round shoulders...
>
> A station-wagon pulled out of a side road, seven plywood coffins strapped on top. At a cafe in the bus terminal we sat next to a young man with two shining claws instead of hands. He was the first of many amputees we were to see over the next couple of days ... We took a yellow taxi ... 'How is San Salvador these days?' we asked the driver innocently, aware that most taxi drivers in El Salvador moonlight as paid informers. 'Muy pacifico', came the confident reply. But every time he stopped at a red light, his head would turn slowly to the left and then the right, and his steady gaze was invariably returned...
>
> Salvadorean television news showed reports of 'guerrilla activity'

in Chalatenango, an area I had hoped to see. Later I learnt that the Salvadorean army ... had fired mortars into the nearby village ... and machine-gunned three women and two small babies. Unable to get to Chalatenango, we went north to Tonacatapeque ... Emerging into the bright sunshine, we found a young man face down in the gutter. We thought he was dead, in El Salvador a fair assumption. But he was merely dead drunk. We then drove southwards, to the beach at La Libertad, to see El Salvador at play ... Just half a mile away was the high black lava field known as El Playon, favoured for years by the death squads as a convenient dumping ground for mutilated bodies...

We went back to San Salvador ... Top on our list of essential visits was the tomb of Archbishop Oscar Romero, gunned down by the army while saying mass in March 1980.[25]

This piece was accompanied by a travel advisory piece on 'Areas to avoid in Central America', in which El Salvador is described as 'one of the most dangerous countries to visit in the region'.

How can we make sense of this ultimate aestheticisation of reality, through which racism and class struggle can be *enjoyed*? The answer should be sought in the nature of tourism itself as a commodity whose value varies enormously, but most especially in its new wafer-thin disguise as a more ethical and moral pastime of the new bourgeoisie. In the last instance, they are persons 'visiting heaps of death and ruin and feeling alive and inspired at the sight'.[26]

References

1   F. Barrett, 'Having a fine time: glad you're not here', *Independent on Sunday* (31 January 1993), p.3.
2   F. Barrett, *The Independent Guide to Real Holidays Abroad 1991* (London, The Independent, 1990).
3   F. Barrett, *The Independent Guide to Real Holidays Abroad 1990* (London, The Independent, 1989).
4   Edward Bruner, 'Of cannibals, tourists, and ethnographers', *Cultural Anthropology* (Vol.4, no.4, 1989), pp.438-45.
5   Katie Wood, 'Belize cleans up in eco-tourism stakes', *Observer* (6 October 1991), p.65.
6   Ibid.
7   Robert Gordon, 'The prospects for anthropological tourism in Bushmanland', *Cultural Survival Quarterly* (Vol.14, no.1, 1990), pp.6-8.
8   See Brian Wheeller, 'Sustaining the ego', *Journal of Sustainable Tourism* (Vol.1, no.2, 1993), pp.121-9.
9   D. Truong, *Sex, Money and Morality: prostitution and tourism in South East Asia* (London, 1991).
10 US Government, Enterprise for the Americas Initiative Act, Dept of Treasury Press Release (27 June 1990).
11 Anita Pleumaron, 'Alternative tourism: a viable solution?', *Contours* (Vol.4, no.8, 1990), pp.12-15.

12 Gordon, op.cit.

13 *Programme for Belize Newsletter*, UK edition (January 1990).

14 Jost Krippendorf, *The Holidaymakers: understanding the impact of leisure and travel* (London, 1987), p.56.

15 See, for example: S. Britton, 'Tourism and economic vulnerability in small Pacific states: the case of Fiji', Development Studies Centre, Monograph No.23 (1981); *Tourism, dependency and development: a mode of analysis*, Occasional Paper No.23 (Canberra, Development Studies Centre, Australian National University, 1981); 'The spatial organisation of tourism in a neo-colonial economy: a Fiji case study', *Pacific Viewpoint* (Vol.21, no.2, 1992), pp.144-65; 'The political economy of tourism in the Third World', *Annals of Tourism Research* (Vol.9), pp.331-58. Also articles by L.A. Perez, 'Aspects of underdevelopment in the West Indies', *Science & Society* (Vol.37, no.4, 1974), pp.473-80; 'Tourism in the West Indies', *Journal of Communications* (Vol.25, 1975), pp.136-43; and H.G. Matthews, 'Radicals and Third World tourism: a Caribbean case', *Annals of Tourism Research* (Vol.5, 1977), pp.20-9.

16 Jean Holder, 'The Caribbean: far greater dependency on tourism likely, *The Courier* (No.122, July/August 1990), pp.74-9.

17 See, for example, D. Truong, op.cit.; P. Holden, J. Horlemann and G. Pfafflin (eds), *Tourism, Prostitution, Development* (Bangkok, Ecumenical Coalition on Third World Tourism, 1983); K. Srisang (ed.), *Caught in Modern Slavery: tourism and child prostitution in Asia* (Bangkok, Ecumenical Coalition on Third World Tourism); P. Phongpaichit, *From Peasant Girls to Bangkok Masseuses* (Geneva, International Labor Office, 1982); P. Nowicka, 'OK for him, but how does she feel?', *Independent on Sunday* (22 December 1991), p.18.

18 Edward Said, *Orientalism* (London, 1991).

19 Kurt Kutay, 'The new ethic in adventure travel', *Buzzworm: The Environmental Journal* (Vol.1, no.4, 1989), pp.31-6.

20 Martha Gellhorn, 'Too good for tourists', *Independent Magazine* (3 November 1990), pp.68-74.

21 James Painter, *Guatemala: false hope, false freedom* (London, 1989).

22 Krippendorf, op.cit.

23 Quoted in *Tourism in Focus* (Autumn, No.2, 1991), p.10.

24 Susan Sontag makes this point about the 'aesthetising tendency of photography', showing how photography 'develops in tandem' with tourism and that, ultimately, the 'medium which conveys distress ends up by neutralising it'. Or, in other words, photographs preserve and consecrate the status quo and 'aesthetise the injuries of class, race and sex' (Susan Sontag, *On Photography* (London, 1979)).

25 Isabel Wolff, 'Weekending in El Salvador', *Independent on Sunday* (27 October 1991), pp.59, 61.

26 Jamaica Kincaid, *A Small Place* (New York, 1988), p.15.

MANNING MARABLE AND LEITH MULLINGS

The divided mind of Black America: race, ideology and politics in the post Civil Rights era*

It is nearly one hundred years since the death of Frederick Douglass and the emergence of Booker T. Washington as the national spokesperson and leader of the African-American community. The Atlanta Compromise address of 1895 by Washington expressed 'in a phraseology acceptable to the dominant elements of the New South – the shift in Negro thought from political to economic action, from immediate integration and protest to self-help, and from rights to duties'.[1] The new contours of racial ideology at the end of the last century were prefigured by the collapse of the first Reconstruction, civil rights and representative democracy across the South, the institutionalisation of the totalitarian repression and violence of Jim Crow, and the confident expansion of capitalism and industrial development across the continent.

In the context of urban America a century later, history repeats itself. Capitalism is once again triumphant, with the destruction of the Soviet model of socialism and the consolidation of the world's economic order on the basis of private markets. The Second Reconstruction, ending with the triumph of the reactionary administration of Ronald Reagan in 1980, culminates in our version of conservative Democrat Grover Cleveland, Bill Clinton. Once again, both parties have turned against the civil rights agenda. And once again, as the race

Manning Marable, professor of history and political science, is director of the Institute for Research in African-American Studies, Columbia University, New York.
Leith Mullings is professor of anthropology at the Graduate Center, City University of New York.
* This paper was presented at the 'Race Matters' conference sponsored at Princeton University, New Jersey, 30 April 1994.

Race & Class, 36, 1 (1994)

searches to find itself, it turns inward, as the voices of both separatism and accommodation grow stronger.

How does 'race' express itself in the contemporary urban site, in the current political conjuncture? And how does the transformation of the political economy express itself in the realignment of racial ideologies?

In the generation since the Civil Rights Movement, there have been many real examples of African-American upward mobility, individual achievement and the growth of a large and increasingly influential African-American middle class. For example, the median incomes of African-American families in which both the wife and the husband were employed rose from about $28,700 in 1967 (in 1990 inflation-adjusted dollars) to over $40,000 in 1990, a real increase of 40 per cent. More than one in seven black families currently earn above $50,000 annually, and thousands of black households now earn over $100,000 annually. Many of these African-American households have moved outside of the central cities into the suburbs, which are predominantly white. Consequently, many of the social, economic and cultural linkages, which previously connected various social classes and organisations, began to erode.

By contrast, since the late 1970s, the general conditions for most of the African-American community have become worse. For example, the percentage of black high school graduates, between the ages of 18 and 26, who go on to college has declined since 1975. The real incomes of younger black workers have fallen sharply during that same period. Standards in health care for millions within the African-American community have fallen, with the black male life expectancy declining to only 64.7 years in 1993. Economically, by 1990, about 12 per cent of all black families were earning less than $5,000 annually. One-third of all African-American families now live below the federal government's poverty level and 46 per cent of all black families are headed by single women. Within the criminal justice system, more than 40 per cent of the 1.4 million prisoners currently incarcerated in federal penitentiaries, prisons and municipal jails of all types are African-Americans. By 1992, 22 per cent of all young African-American men between the ages of 20 and 29 were in prison, on probation, parole or awaiting trial. In New York City alone, the percentage of young black men within the penal and criminal justice system was 31 per cent.

Two key elements explaining the socioeconomic dilemmas millions of African-American families are experiencing are: (1) the deep structural crisis of the economies in major American cities, in which thousands of businesses and corporations have divested and relocated, either to the suburbs or outside of the country; and (2) the fiscal crisis of the federal, state and local governments, in which the resources to fund social programmes have been significantly reduced. Throughout the decade of the 1980s, black communities throughout the country have experienced massive increases in homelessness and unemployment, a proliferation of instances of deadly violence, and a deterioration in the quality of public education, public health care facilities and public transportation.

*　　*　　*

It is within this difficult context that the current generation of African-American leaders must be judged. Thirty years ago, during the height of Jim Crow segregation, the number of elected black officials nationwide was barely one hundred; the number of African-Americans in Congress was five, and the number of blacks serving as mayors of US cities and towns of all sizes was zero. Today, forty African-Americans sit in the US Congress; more than forty African-Americans are mayors, and over 8,000 blacks have been elected to government positions. Yet these major increases in the number of black representatives cannot be equated with a parallel rise of leverage or clout within the political system.

There are several reasons for this disparity. First, despite the massive increase in black representation, African-Americans today still only account for 2 per cent of all elected and appointed officials throughout the nation. In dozens of counties having substantial black constituencies, there are few or no African-American elected officials. Blacks still remain under-represented within the electoral structure of power and decision-making.

Second, in many instances, African-American elected officials have what might be termed 'responsibility without authority'. Many black mayors, for instance, exercise relatively little control or authority over local governmental bureaucracies. They have few levers of power by which they can distribute goods, services or positions of influence to their supporters. In some cases, this has contributed to a sense of political disillusionment among sectors of the African-American electorate and a decline in voter registration and political participation rates.

Elsewhere, the question of black leadership is challenged by the recent emergence of what could be termed 'post-black politics' – that is, the rise of African-American political candidates who have relatively few connections with organic black social and political formations and institutions, and consciously minimise their identity as 'minority' or 'black'. The background of 'post-black politics' was created by another dimension of US political behaviour – the regrettable, yet unavoidable, fact that the vast majority of white voters generally will not cast ballots for a black, first-time candidate for public office, regardless of her or his party label, ideology or history of civic involvements. Until 1989, no first-time African-American mayoral candidate had earned more than 30 per cent of the white vote – in effect, a 'racial ceiling' blacks had failed to overcome. Whites' refusal to support black candidates was particularly apparent in urban areas and in cities where blacks or other racial minorities represented substantial shares of the overall electorate.

By contrast, blacks as a group continued to exhibit 'non-racial' electoral behaviour, that is, voting overwhelmingly for white candidates whose views on public policy they support over black candidates who embraced conservative or Republican positions. For instance, in the recent mayoral election in New York City, 95 per cent of all black voters supported incumbent candidate David Dinkins and gave over 90 per cent of their vote to the mayor's white Democratic running mates for city-wide offices. Such a constituency was nowhere present among the city's white Democratic voters, who rejected Dinkins by a margin of nearly four to one.

Some black elected officials who encountered this inevitable 'race ceiling' in politics began, by the late 1980s, to minimise or downplay their racial identity or affiliations with institutions within the African-American community. Candidates began to run for public office who 'happened to be black', or who refused to be identified as 'black politicians'. Some of the more successful politicians representing this 'deracialised politics' included mayor Michael White of Cleveland, mayor Norm Rice of Seattle and Virginia governor Douglas Wilder. To be sure, the development of a deracialised current of black politics represents a successful culmination of the racial philosophy of integration. After all, it was Dr Martin Luther King Jr who articulated the hope that African-Americans would be judged 'not by the color of [their] skin, but by the content of [their] character'. The irony of racial inequality in the 1990s is that, while this statement certainly expresses a long-term aspiration of the black freedom movement, it cannot grasp or address the tragic spirit of class inequality, poverty, unemployment, violence and social destruction that is manifestly represented in *racial* terms. Race and institutional racism have not yet declined in significance.

Compounding this sense of social class and vocational division within the black community is yet another growing schism, a deepening division of culture, values and social relations. To a real extent, the cultural clash is intergenerational, symbolised by the radical differences in discourse, political experiences and social expectations between those African-Americans born before 1964 and those who were born after the great legislative victories of the Civil Rights Movement. Simplistically, one might describe this great division as being between the 'We Shall Overcome' generation and the 'Hip-Hop' generation. The former lived through the most dynamic and icon-shattering decade of the twentieth century, the 1960s. This earlier generation witnessed the collapse of Jim Crow, the growth of a vast black middle class and professional/political elite, the rise and fall of Black Power, the leadership of Malcolm and Martin, and the eruption of social revolutions across Africa and the Caribbean. This turbulent history left indelible marks on the political culture and group psychology of this earlier generation. For those who stood streets – defiantly facing Alabama state troopers at the Edmund Pettus bridge in Selma in 1965; or seizing student union buildings and dormitories at dozens of white college campuses to force recalcitrant administrations to initiate Black Studies departments; or who registered hundreds of thousands of new voters, from the Mississippi Delta to Chicago's sprawling South Side – the possibilities in politics were only limited by the boundaries of our imaginations. Everything seemed possible for a brief, shining moment. Real incomes for black families had increased dramatically from 1945 to 1975; the number of African-Americans enrolled in colleges and post-secondary schools had soared from 40,000 to nearly 700,000 in only thirty years. Tomorrow would always be better than yesterday.

The 'Hip-Hop' generation's primary experience in politics can be characterised by one word, defeat. This generation's most dominating and influential national political figure was president Ronald Reagan. The generation which produced the dynamic cultural expression of rap music came to maturity in a context of rising black-on-black violence, symbolised by the Crips vs the Bloods in south central Los Angeles; during the next five years, more black people were to be killed in our central cities than the total number of American troops who were killed during the Vietnam war. Hip-Hop emerged in the context of widespread unemployment, homelessness and the omnipresence of fear and social alienation. For many of our young people, there is no sense or expectation that a future is worth living for, or that it even exists. One lives for today, because tomorrow might never come.

We live in New York City, and the full dimensions of the crisis of race and class for the current generation of African-Americans throughout urban America are apparent to anyone. In New York City, between 1980 and 1992, 87,000 private sector jobs were lost. During the same years, the number of African-Americans living below the poverty level increased from 520,000 to 664,000 people. The average black family in New York City now earns $24,000 annually, compared to over $40,000 per year for whites. Black adult male unemployment rates are officially 13 per cent, but actual labour force participation rates of adults in Harlem and Bedford-Stuyvesant, within the formal sector of the economy, are below 60 per cent.

The criminal justice system has become the chief means for regulating the vast supply of unemployed, under-educated, young black workers. In central Harlem alone, 2,500 young people were arrested in 1992. Ninety-five per cent of those in jail in New York City are African-Americans and Latinos. Who makes up this prison population? Ninety per cent lack a high school diploma; more than one-half have less than a sixth-grade level of educational ability. Two-thirds of all young black people who are in jail are awaiting trial, at an average cost of $150 per day. The average pretrial detention in New York City is fifty days, costing $7,900 per prisoner. Tens of millions of dollars are wasted to warehouse unemployed labour: the American version of the 'gulag archipelago'. Nationwide, our prison population is expected to double within the next six years. One recent estimate predicted that, at current growth rates, by the year 2053, there will be more Americans of all races *inside* prison than *outside*.

The most tragic casualties of the race/class crisis in our cities today, however, are the children. In the area of health care, six out of ten preschool children in New York City are not immunised. There are currently only ninety-six nurses for the 600 elementary schools throughout the city. Every day in New York, 70,500 children use drugs; thirty-five babies are born at low birth weights. More than 160,000 children, mostly African-American and Latino, have no health insurance. And today, AIDS is the leading cause of death in New York City for children under the age of 5. In the area of housing and home-lessness, New York currently has about 90,000 homeless people, 90 per cent of whom are black and Hispanic. Tonight, 24,000 people, including nearly 10,000 children, will sleep in city-run homeless shelters. During the next five years, one out of every twelve black children in New York City will sleep in a homeless shelter.

*   *   *

We are, in effect, in a new historical period: the intensification of race and class inequalities in our cities, the social class polarisation within the African-American community, the fragmentation and confusion of black leadership, the quiet contempt for black interests expressed by both major parties. How have black intellectuals responded to the new period and, more specifically, what is the social responsibility of the African-American intelligentsia?

In study in progress on the theme 'Identity, inequality and power', we are attempting to chart the shifting currents of contemporary racial ideology within America. We believe that today within the black community there are essentially three overlapping, strategic visions about the nature of the contemporary political economy, the meaning of 'race' in the post-Civil Rights era and what is to be done in the next century to address the problems of black people. These three strategic visions may be termed 'inclusion' or 'pragmatic integrationism', 'separatism' or 'racial autonomy' and 'transformation' or 'radical multicultural democracy'. Each of these currents has evolved from long historical and ideological traditions within African-American life. Let us discuss the contemporary and historical examples of each; their assumptions, goals and ideological perspectives; their respective social bases or core constituencies; and the conditions under which they exert influence and authority within the African-American population. The Marable/Mullings model of racial ideology suggests three overlapping spheres of political culture, ideology and social forces, not distinctly separate parties or tendencies. And by themselves, such models are inherently limited. They explain some things and not others. The great majority of African-American people find themselves located at the conjunctural centre of these three great visions; they may favour 'nationalism', 'integration' or the demands of 'radical democracy' to varying degrees at different times, depending upon the racial attitudes of the white majority, the state of the economy and other factors.

The 'inclusionist' vision incorporates the traditional integrationist perspective of the earlier twentieth century, but also neo-liberal and pragmatic currents of the post-Civil Rights period. The inclusionist vision implicitly assumes that African-Americans are basically 'Americans who happen to be black'; it calls for the eradication of all sites of racial particularity and social isolation; it seeks affirmation and legitimacy within the state and civil society for American capitalism and it works within established institutions to influence public policy. The historical roots of the inclusionist position are found in the aspirations of the free Negro communities of the North before the Civil War, in the politics of Walter White, Roy Wilkins, the younger Du Bois and the older A. Philip Randolph. Its social base is found within the black middle class, the professional and managerial elite, public sector employees and elements of the stable blue-collar working class in the cities. The inclusionist vision is expressed ideologically as pragmatic liberalism, although, with the expansion of a class-conscious black elite in the 1970s and 1980s, theorists such as Shelby Steele and economist Thomas Sowell have emerged which reflect the growing opportunism and materialism within this stratum. Pragmatic liberalism as an ideology is best expressed in the social science literature of William Julius Wilson; in the humanities, its most prominent representative is my friend and colleague, Henry Louis Gates. In the *New York Times* recently, Gates denounced racial separatists such as Khalid Abdul Muhammad as 'calculating demagogues', criticised narrowly-based 'identity politics' and called for 'a liberalism of heart and spine'.[2] The inclusionist position gains strength when the state and white civil society create opportunities for the articulation and expression of blacks' grievances, and when there is a sense of political optimism which is pervasive within the African-American community. The chief difficulty for the inclusionist vision is that, despite the concrete victories in the legal and political sphere for blacks and the growth of a professional and managerial elite, the actual material conditions for

the majority of black people have grown clearly worse in the last fifteen
years. The overwhelming crisis of race and class in our cities and the
retreat by white liberals from their previous advocacy of blacks'
interests undermine the legitimacy of inclusionist politics.

In reverse, yet mirror-like, opposition to inclusionism is the
separatist vision of race relations. The orientation of black nationalism
assumes that 'race' is a historically fixed category, which will not
magically decline in significance over time; it suggests that blacks must
define themselves within their own autonomous cultural context; and
it is deeply pessimistic about the ability or willingness of white civil
society to transform itself democratically to include the demands of
people of colour. Culturally, it suggests that African-Americans are
African people who happen to speak English and live in America. Or,
as Malcolm X once declared: 'Just because a cat has its kittens in an
oven, you don't call the kittens biscuits.' There is a subterranean unity
between inclusionist and separatist visions; one usually advances in
influence within black political culture when the other retreats.

The historical roots of the separatist perspective can be traced to the
maroon impulse of runaway slaves, in the creation of all-black towns
such as Mound Bayou, Mississippi, in 1887, or the back-to-Africa ideas
of Martin Delany. In the early twentieth century, separatism was best
expressed in a mass movement by the Universal Negro Improvement
Association of Marcus Garvey and, subsequently, within the Nation
of Islam of Elijah Muhammad. The separatist explosion of the 1960s
gave us numerous tendencies of black nationalism: the revolutionary
nationalism of the League of Revolutionary Black Workers in Detroit
and the Black Panther Party in Oakland; the neo-Booker T.
Washington, black-capitalist nationalism of Roy Innis and Floyd
McKissick of the Congress of Racial Equality; the cultural nationalism
of Maulana Karenga and Amiri Baraka, the establishment of rituals
such as Kwanzaa; and the political nationalism manifested in the Gary
Black Convention of 1972 and the National Black Political Assembly.
The primary social base for nationalism today comes from the Hip-
Hop generation, the marginalised African-American working class and
a strong segment of the entrepreneurial black elite. On 125th Street in
Harlem, for example, one can observe the nationalism of the market-
place, or 'vendor nationalism'; racial solidarity and 'buy black' senti-
ment is utilised for capital formation.

Among the many separatist currents of today, the most scholarly
and influential is Afrocentrism: its chief representatives would include
Temple University African-American Studies head Molefi Asante,
City College Black Studies chair Len Jefferies and Lincoln University
president Niara Sudarkasa. Unlike the inclusionists, the nationalists
have always understood the absolutely essential connections between
culture, identity and politics: one's sense of history, the practising of

Commentary

Palestine

The economic fist in the political glove

In an article in the Israeli daily *Haaretz,*[1] Israeli political analyst, Meron Benvenisti, argues that the 'success' of the PLO/Israeli peace agreement was only made possible by its 'deliberate ambiguity'. In the Declaration of Principles (DOP) signed in Washington on 13 September 1993, he says, can be read two mutually exclusive political visions. For the PLO, the DOP is 'the first step' in the 'theory of stages' by which 'a national authority will be established in any area of liberated Palestine'. For the Israeli government, however, the DOP is the final political realisation of former defence minister and architect of the 1967 occupation, Moshe Dayan; a classic 'functional compromise' strategy, where Palestinians of the territories are granted 'administrative authority within municipal boundaries', while the Israelis keep a firm grip on all matters pertaining to security and the region's resources.

Hence, says Benvenisti, the symbolically explosive nature of the 'border question' in the current PLO/Israeli negotiations on implementing self rule, and why its resolution or otherwise 'may even determine whether the agreement is implemented'. Control of border crossings pits the two conflicting visions against each other and forces them out of ambiguity and into the cold, clear air. If the PLO, however emblematically, wrest some kind of authority over borders, then what they have signed with the DOP is the rudiments of an international entity, or sovereignty in its incipient stage. For the Israelis, 'owning the fence' strikes at the very meaning of Palestinian self rule which, by their lights, is and must remain a wholly 'internal arrangement'. 'Control of external security', Israeli foreign minister Shimon Peres told president Mitterand in Paris on 16 December 1993, 'is the most important difference between autonomy and an independent Palestinian state.'[2]

Benvenisti probably overplays his hand a little. One should not underestimate both the PLO and Israel's facility for resolving one ambiguity by substituting it for another. Yet he is right to point out the essentially political nature of the dispute, with both sides waging a war of attrition to extract from the DOP entirely alternative scenarios for self rule.

This is something that cannot be said about the economic debates so far thrown up by the agreement. Unlike the fraught issues of borders, settlements, refugees and even the size of Jericho, the future of the Palestinian economy during the 'interim phase of self rule' is bathed in the rare light of PLO/Israeli unanimity. On his return from Paris, Peres let it be known that 'the Palestinians agree with us today on creating a market economy, an open economy with no borders, with free movement of goods and trade between the two of us',[3] while chief of the PLO delegation Nabil Sha'th, on the eve of the Washington signing, gushed that the DOP means 'a full peace with Israel, with totally open borders' which will 'create with Israel an economic community for the whole Middle East'.[4]

'Open borders', 'a Middle East economic community' and the like are politically-loaded terms that, since 13 September, have been, in both Israeli and PLO discourses, voided of all political content. Yet the DOP is primarily an economic document. Two-thirds of it is devoted to describing the functions of eight PLO/Israeli 'liaison committees' whose job it is to harness, in Sha'th's words, a degree of 'mutual economic interest that exceeds any agreement signed between the two states' (sic).[5] A less charitable interpretation has described the DOP thus: 'It's political divorce and economic marriage. The Palestinians have negotiated a partnership with the Israelis for developing their own economic affairs.'[6] Whatever the PLO has signed in the DOP, the strategic question of Palestine's future economic relations with Israel lies, or should lie, at the heart of any Palestinian political vision for statehood.

Palestinian critics of the agreement base their critique less on the economic stipulations adumbrated by the DOP – for these are so nebulous as to be 'almost vacuous' – than on the rosy vistas sketched by people like Sha'th and Peres. Perhaps the most trenchant advocate of this line is the head of Gaza's Economic Development Group, Salah Abdl Shafi. Neither an apologist for the agreement nor an 'ideological rejectionist' of it, Abdl Shafi counts himself among that growing band of Palestinian intellectuals (like his father, former Palestinian delegation head, Haidar Abdl Shafi, Edward Said, Mahmoud Darwish and others) who view the DOP as both politically irreversible and, in Mouin Rabbani's words, as 'deeply flawed and potentially fatal to Palestinian national aspirations'.[7]

If Abdl Shafi agrees with Sha'th that the *sine qua non* of Israel's new relationship with the occupied territories will be 'totally open borders' rather than military subjugation, this for him spells not so much 'reconciliation and cooperation' as Palestine's final and 'absolute incorporation into the Israeli economy' and, with it, the vanquishing of 'any notion of developing a genuinely independent Palestinian economic sector'.[8]

Gaza's new economic arrangement

The DOP sets the political seal of approval on a new economic dispensation that the Israelis have assiduously been carving out in Gaza for the last three years and which, with the agreement, they now plan to extend to the territories as a whole. The 'new arrangement' had its germ in a series of reports on the Gazan economy written in the early 1990s by Israeli economist Ezra Sadan, described by the Israeli press as 'a champion of Greater Israel in his politics, but a neo-liberal when it comes to economics'.[9]

In the wake of the Gulf war, Israel's perceived 'security need' was to staunch the flow of Palestinian labour across the Green Line, running at the time at around 30,000 to 40,000 workers from Gaza and about 100,000 from the territories as a whole. However, Sadan's remit was not so much to lessen Gaza's chronic dependency on the Israeli economy[10] as, in Abdl Shafi's words, 'to re-structure the relations of that dependency... The means of this dependency were not, as had been the case historically during the occupation, via a daily migration of mass Palestinian labour into Israel. Rather, the new vehicle was a system of sub-contracting between Palestinian capital and sectors of Israel capital.'

In terms of labour, the Israelis have clearly been successful in their desires. By the time of the peace agreement, the number of Palestinian workers from Gaza entering Israel on any day was down to 20,000. Abdl Shafi lists three other spheres of the Gazan economy where the new arrangement has also taken hold. 'In August 1991, the military governor issued order 1055 which aims to "encourage investment in the Gaza Strip". Generally speaking, this liberalised the licensing of firms so that it became much easier for Palestinians to engage in investment activity.'

In practice, however, licences were granted selectively to Palestinian outfits whose trade was entirely dependent on Israeli contractors. Nor did the move open up competition with Israel. 'While such (newly licensed) Palestinian firms may threaten certain "unviable" companies in Israel,' says Abdl Shafi, 'it certainly cannot challenge entire sectors, given the difference in scale between the two economies.' On the contrary, as Palestinian economist Adel Samara points out, what the new relationship actually portends is 'the swallowing of the economies of the Palestinian cantons' (like the Gaza Strip) 'and converting them into components of the Israeli economy, but with an Arab face'.[11]

In addition, since 1991, Israel has imposed a number of punitive measures on Gaza's agricultural sector, whose economic effect has been to thwart its traditional citrus and vegetable production in favour of the manufacture of ornamentals or flowers. Citrus is the single biggest income earner of all economic activities in the Gaza Strip, with export routes to Europe and the Gulf countries. As a result of Israeli confiscations, however, the amount of arable citrus land in Gaza has shrunk from 75,000 to 53,000 dunums. But Israel's purpose here is not merely territorial. Rather, it is to decouple Gaza's trade with other economies, the better to lock it firmly into Israel's own. According to the head of the Strip's Citrus Producers' Union, Hashem Shawa, of the 9,000 tonnes of citrus harvested in Gaza in 1993, '90 per cent was sold to Israeli juice factories' and at a 'captive' price so cheap that it 'hardly covered the farmers' production costs'.[12] A further means of 'deepening dependency', says Abdl Shafi, is to encourage single crop sectors like flowers. 'Israel is a major exporter of flowers to Europe, but production costs there are high because Israeli labour is expensive. So, by shifting production to the Strip, the Israelis reduce substantially their labour costs whilst maintaining their market share in Europe because – it goes without saying – all of the export routes open to Gaza's flowers are in the hands of Israeli contractors.'

While the Strip's agricultural base has, in Sadan's parlance, been 'encouraged' to 'degenerate',[13] 140 industrialised greenhouses have been constructed in the last eighteen months whose output is wholly geared to ornamentals. 'In addition,' says Abdl Shafi, 'our strawberry yield is now totally dependent on exclusive export to Israel.' All the signs are that, with the agreement, this will be Israel's agrarian game-plan for the territories as a whole. At the 'economic committee' talks held in Paris in October, for example, Israeli negotiators signalled that Israel was 'ready' to lift the prohibitive tax burdens on Palestinian agricultural producers and, on 16 December, Peres announced that his government 'would ultimately end its twenty-six-year ban on allowing Palestinians to freely export their farm produce to Israel'.[14]

Finally, the Israelis have set about establishing what Sadan calls 'industrial parks' throughout the Gaza Strip. These parks are modelled on similar projects set up in countries like Taiwan and Mexico.[15] They amount, says Abdl Shafi, to 'pockets of infrastructure surrounded by deserts of underdevelopment':

Sadan said that because the task of developing an economic

infrastructure for the whole of the territories would 'cost billions', Israel should instead concentrate on providing business facilities like electrification and telecommunications for industry alone, sited on small parks. These parks would be made up of small Palestinian and Israeli sub-contracting firms which would be umbilically tied to the Israeli economy. Remember that Sadan was writing before Gaza/ Jericho First and before the arrival on the scene of the World Bank, whose infrastructural prescriptions for the territories, by the way, fit him like a glove.

Israel has just opened Gaza's first industrial park in the Beit Hanoun district, is busy constructing another and has laid plans for a third. There are similar moves afoot, says Abdl Shafi, to establish a 'network of parks' in the West Bank.

Unlevel playing fields and closed borders

Against this backdrop, the PLO leadership's zealous embrace of the 'free market' appears not only uncritical but catastrophic, especially if, in the words of PLO executive member Yassir Abed Rabbo, the new Palestinian entity 'wants to forge the strongest possible economic links with Jordan and our Arab surroundings'.[16] Abdl Shafi explains why:

> If the new Palestinian authority wants to pursue a policy of genuine, or even partial, disengagement from the Israeli economy, it will have to offer Palestinian farmers, businessmen and sub-contractors a real economic alternative. But if, as certain PLO and Israeli economists say, this is going to be left to the free market, then this class will obviously choose the Israelis. First, because the mutual relations are already established and, second, because, come the 'peace', Israeli contractors can guarantee them authentic export markets.

A like argument obtains with the PLO's currently unproblematic commitment to 'open borders' which, as Abdl Shafi warns, in reality will be open for the Israelis to penetrate Arab markets but closed to the Palestinians to trade in any market other than Israel's. Only now, under 'self rule', the 'veto' will not be imposed by military diktat but, rather, through economic imperative:

> If there is one point that unites all shades of Israeli political opinion about the agreement, it is that there must be 'open borders' between Israel and the new Palestinian entity. While direct taxation can be in the hands of the PLO authority, they say, indirect taxation or VAT will have to be standardised. But if Palestinians are made to buy and sell at Israeli prices, we may as well forget Jordan or any other Arab market for that matter. And this 'trade disadvantage' would be reinforced, not lessened, if, in the wake of the agreement, there is

peace and economic normalisation between Israel and the Arabs. Gaza, for example, simply cannot compete with an economy that in terms of GNP is currently ten times its own size. As with most 'free markets', this is not a level playing field.

If Abdl Shafi's prognoses sound unduly alarmist to those who follow Israel's and the PLO leadership's largely Panglossian vision of the 'economy under self rule', they nevertheless strike a chord with Israel's business community. According to Israeli journalist Asher Davidi, the consensus among Israel's capitalist class is that the DOP marks the beginning of 'a transition from colonialism to neo-colonialism'[17] in Israel's economic dealings with the territories. The tableaux Abdl Shafi paints on sub-contracting, agriculture, tax standardisation, industry and labour are enthusiastically endorsed by Israel's manufacturers and financiers and represent 'positions that are acceptable to the Rabin government'. 'Israel's policy is clear,' says Davidi. 'As Lieutenant-Colonel Hilel Sheinfeld, the Israeli coordinator of operations in the territories, put it, the declared goal of his work is to "integrate the economy of the territories into the Israeli economy".'[18]

The political form of 'integration' is ultimately less significant than its economic prize. 'It's not important whether there will be a Palestinian state, autonomy or a Palestinian-Jordanian federation,' says president of the Israeli Industrialists' Association Dov Lautman. 'The economic borders between Israel and the territories must remain open.'[19]

If the current PLO leadership really has given up on any belief in economic self-determination, then, in Edward Said's words, 'most Palestinians in the territories, economically speaking, will almost certainly remain where they are'.[20] Abdl Shafi agrees. He predicts two distinct economic phases for the interim period of self rule. In the short term (for 'security reasons'), Israel will maintain the economic siege of the West Bank and Gaza, sustaining thereby a vast 'reserve pool of cheap labour' on which both 'Palestinian and Israeli sub-contractors can draw at minimal cost' and through which the 'new economic arrangement' can be consolidated.[21] In the long term, if there is 'peace', the blockade will be quietly lifted, which means that 'between 100,000 and 120,000 Palestinian workers' will still have to go for work inside the Green Line. In the first phase, structural unemployment rates in Gaza will stick at their current averages of 40 per cent overall and 60 per cent in the refugee camps.[22] In the second, the rate would decrease to around 20 per cent. This, Israeli army analysts inform us, is 'entirely manageable from a security point of view'. But, in both cases, says Abdl Shafi, 'we will be working for Israel. Maybe now we will be working for them in Gaza and the West Bank rather more than in Tel Aviv or Ashkelon or Beersheva. But we will be working for them nonetheless.'

Should Abdl Shafi's forewarnings be anywhere near the mark,

then Palestinian debates on the economy under 'self rule' will have to move away from the finer points of how best to stake out 'coalitions between Israeli and Palestinian capital', and on to, as Adel Samara puts it, more mundane and 'class' matters like 'labour, wages, rights and safety'.[23] Otherwise, for the mass of Palestinians in the (economically) occupied territories, the understanding is likely to dawn that, as Edward Said says, 'much more important than having a state is the kind of state it is'.[24]

Gaza GRAHAM USHER
January 1994

References

1 'Border conflict', *Haaretz* (16 December 1993).
2 Quoted in *Haaretz* (15 December 1993).
3 'Peres: Israel, PLO agree on open market', *Jerusalem Post* (17 December 1993).
4 'The breakthrough: waiting for the word "withdraw"', *Jerusalem Post* (3 September 1993).
5 Ibid.
6 Mark Taylor, Research Officer, UNWRA, Gaza Strip. Interview with author.
7 Mouin Rabbani, '"Gaza-Jericho first": the Palestinian debate', *Middle East International* (24 September 1993).
8 Interview with author. All quotations from Abdl Shafi are from an interview I held with him in October 1993. The full text is published in *Middle East Report* (January-February 1994).
9 'Investing in peace', *Jerusalem Post* (14 May 1993). The reports referred to are Sadan's *A policy for immediate economic-industrial development in the Gaza Strip* (Ben-Ezra Consultants, August 1991) and *Durable employment for the refugee-populated region of Gaza* (April 1993).
10 According to Edward Said, 'over 80 per cent of the West Bank and Gaza economy is dependent on Israel'. See his 'The morning after', *London Review of Books* (21 October 1993).
11 Adel Samara, 'Israel swallowing the economy of Palestinian cantons', *News from Within* (5 October 1993).
12 Hisham Shawa, 'Letter to the Arab League' *Al Quds* (6 January 1994).
13 Ezra Sadan, *A policy for immediate economic-industrial development...*, op.cit.
14 'Peres: Israel, PLO agree on an open market', op.cit.
15 For a theoretical analysis of the role of 'industrial parks' in the 'new imperialism', see A. Sivanandan, 'New circuits of imperialism' in *Communities of Resistance: writings on black struggles for socialism* (London, 1990).
16 'PLO wary of Israel's economic plans', *Jerusalem Post* (23 September 1993).
17 Asher Davidi, 'Israel's economic strategy for Palestinian independence', *Middle East Report* (September-October 1993).
18 Ibid.
19 Ibid.
20 'The morning after', op.cit.
21 For the political background to Israel's closure of the occupied territories, see my 'Why Gaza says yes, mostly' in *Race & Class* (January-March 1994).
22 Mark Taylor, op.cit.
23 'Israel swallowing the economy of the Palestinian cantons', op.cit.
24 'The morning after', op.cit.

El Salvador

Birth of a new culture

Whether the transformation of El Salvador into a representative democracy is the product of a genuine social and political evolution or a tactical manoeuvre by its ruling elite as the result of outside pressure, there is no doubt that the country is now enjoying a degree of political freedom unprecedented in its history. One of the positive consequences of the changed political climate has been a revival of the country's cultural and intellectual life, after more than a decade of repression and civil war in which it virtually ceased to exist. Since the end of the war, writers, actors and musicians have begun to re-establish themselves in the country after spending years in exile. Others have emerged from clandestinity and 'internal exile', or come from former guerrilla bases in the mountains to take advantage of the political liberties enshrined in the Chapultepec Peace Accords. For the first time in more than a decade, it has become possible to engage in public intellectual debate without fear of being killed or disappeared. New magazines and newspapers have been established and another is soon to appear. In new nightclubs like La Luna – 'a locale open to space, time and the imagination' – an unlikely clientele, containing former guerrilla *commandantes* and the sons and daughters of the bourgeoisie, enjoys a weekly range of cultural activities including poetry readings, concerts and dance performances.

All this amounts to something of a cultural boom and would have been unimaginable only a few years ago, when the energies of the society were largely devoted to war and survival and culture was not a high priority. 'During the war, the cultural movement in El Salvador disappeared completely,' said Fernando Umana, artistic director of the theatre company, Sol del Rio, 'the country shut itself off. The majority of artists went into exile, while those who remained were like those animals who live underground, working in complete isolation for fear of being labelled subversives.'

El Salvador's oldest and most prestigious theatre group, Sol del Rio went into exile in 1981, living and working in Mexico and Europe before returning to the country in 1989. Since 1992, the group has been involved in its most successful work to date, *San Salvador After the Eclipse*, to enthusiastic receptions from both rural and urban audiences. *San Salvador After the Eclipse* is without doubt the country's first major artistic achievement of the postwar period, and is a powerful and moving piece of theatre by any standards. Based on an Argentinian play about the aftermath of the Malvinas war, the original play has been completely reworked and rewritten in the Salvadoran context by Salvadoran playwright Carlos Velis, with further input from the group itself and the audiences who attended the first rehearsals. The result is an entirely new play, which brilliantly illuminates the hopes and dilemmas of postwar Salvadoran society and analyses the destructive impact of the war. Set in a poor neighbourhood in San Salvador, the plot describes the reunion of two couples, survivors of El Salvador's revolutionary generation, shortly after the signing of the Peace Accords. One of the couples has spent the war in exile in the United States, while the other has remained in San Salvador, and the reunion reveals the conflicting attitudes and expectations to the past, the future and El Salvador itself.

Out of these basic dramatic ingredients, Velis and Sol del Rio have constructed a play that manages to be funny, painful and nostalgic, and which addresses the complex issues of national reconciliation and national identity with great intelligence and moral passion. The play's fundamental message is clear: that no matter how destructive and horrific the past has been, the 'eclipse' of reason and humanity during the war must be transcended by a new spirit of tolerance and reconciliation. In this sense, the play reflects the tentative optimism that has made the peace process in El Salvador possible in the first place. The groups themselves see both the play itself and their theatrical work in general as vehicles for promoting national reconciliation, and have recently been performing *San Salvador After the Eclipse* in the former conflict zones as part of a project financed by the Danish government. As Fernando explains, 'After the war, the population is a little sceptical about the possibility of a better future. As a theatre group, we feel that we can make a contribution towards national reconciliation by giving people hope.'

With the resurgence in death squad activity, soaring rates of criminal violence and the deepening poverty of the majority of the population all threatening the fragile political consensus in El Salvador, the optimistic note on which the play concludes may yet prove to be premature. Yet, by giving artistic expression to the debates that are taking place in Salvadoran households throughout the country, *San Salvador After the Eclipse* exactly captures the mood of a traumatised society as it seeks to recover from the most terrible period in its history.

The fact that such a play can even be performed at all is itself an indication of the new freedom of expression that Salvadoran writers have begun to take advantage of. After more than fifty years of direct or indirect military rule, in which any form of dissidence was often violently suppressed, even former guerrillas are now able to publish openly. 'Not only do we have political spaces that we didn't have before,' says novelist, journalist and short-story writer Horacio

Castellanos Moya, 'but we haven't begun to make the most of them because we haven't the means. We don't have the magazines and publications that could allow writers to participate in the construction of a democratic culture.'

A fellow-traveller of the FMLN in the early 1980s, Castellanos Moya spent most of the war in exile in Mexico, before returning to El Salvador in 1990. Today, he is the editor of *Tendencias*, a new political and cultural magazine which is intended to promote 'pluralism, tolerance, clarity, and a critical attitude'. Apart from the centre-left newspaper, *Diario Latino*, and the excellent publications produced by the Jesuit university, *Tendencias* remains one of the few outlets for intellectual debate on political and cultural issues available in El Salvador. Elsewhere, TV, radio and the abysmal mainstream press are largely subservient to the ruling ARENA party, and the student anti-communist tirades that continue to pour forth from newspapers like *La Prensa Grafica* are a depressing indication of how little the Right has accommodated itself to the changed political situation.

The fostering of a democratic culture able to accommodate a variety of differing opinions is no easy task in a still-polarised country that has barely begun to emerge from a horrendous civil war. In the opinion of Castellanos Moya, the polarisation of Salvadoran society which followed the fraudulent military election victory in 1972 will take some time to overcome. 'There's no tradition of an authentic intellectual class in this country, in the sense of providing independent critical thinking and analysis. What we've had instead are ideologues and organic intellectuals who have put themselves at the service of one side or another. The war made critical thinking impossible, you could only criticise the enemy, never your own side. Those of us who left the country had a certain distance from the war, but those who were directly involved in it have found it difficult to adjust to the change.' While the politicisation of Salvadoran letters has produced great writers like Roque Dalton and Manlio Argueta, it has also favoured a particular kind of committed, partisan literature which many Salvadoran writers feel is no longer appropriate to the reality of the country. For the revolutionary Left of the 1960s and 1970s, convinced that it was on the verge of a historic transformation of Salvadoran society, the task of writers and intellectuals was to contribute towards the final victory by producing literature that conformed to 'objective' scientific truths about society and which reflected the historical experience of the most dispossessed sectors of the population. The outbreak of the war reinforced the tendency to regard artistic production as an extension of the political struggle taking place. With their margin of independence reduced to virtually nil by repression from the Right and the aesthetic regimentation demanded by the Left, Salvadoran writers were obliged to take sides or leave the country.

'Before the Peace Accords, we lived in a manichean schematic world,' explains Geovanni Galdeas. 'There were only two possibilities – reaction or revolution, black and white, with no variations in between – and you could only be one or the other.'

Like many of the younger generation of writers who grew up in the 1970s, Galdeas gravitated towards the Left and participated in the war as a member of the ERP, one of the five organisations in the FMLN. In 1985, after actively participating in the war, he became disillusioned with the revolution and the war, partly as a result of the brutal sectarian murder of the FMLN commander, 'Ana Maria', by her own party comrades. Unable to continue living in the country, he went into exile in Mexico, where he still lives today, alternating between Mexico City and El Salvador. One of his plays, *The Lecture*, deals with one of the most shameful chapters in the history of the Left, the 'execution' of the poet, Roque Dalton, by his own comrades in the ERP in 1974. The satirical criticism of the Left which the play contains would certainly have been seen as breaking ranks before the end of the war, nor would the play have been any more acceptable to the Right. Today, however, the Sol del Rio is preparing to perform the play in San Salvador for the first time. In Galdeas' opinion, the end of the war has brought a new creative freedom to Salvadoran literature which he believes will produce a new kind of writing, distinct from the politicised, socially-committed literature of the postwar period. 'The principal tendency of postwar writing, however incipient at the moment, is the diversity of voices and positions. Instead of war songs and slogans there are small, individual voices, expressing their confusion and disorientation, and I think this will produce a more humanised literature.'

$$*\quad*\quad*$$

The retreat from the social terrain towards the private concerns of the individual is a fairly generalised feature of Salvadoran society in the postwar period and is perhaps a natural sequel to a period of great social upheaval. While the disenchantment with politics and ideology is by no means unique to El Salvador, it has a particular resonance in a country which is in the process of recovering from a catastrophic political and military confrontation, whose results do not correspond to the enormous sacrifices required to achieve them. Shortly before his death, the murdered Jesuit intellectual Ignacio Ellacuria identified the abandonment by the Left of its utopian aspirations as one of the factors that made a negotiated solution to the war possible. But while there is almost universal relief that the war has ended, there is little sign of enthusiasm for the political order which has emerged in its wake. 'I think that a lot of Salvadorans are disoriented by the speed of the changes that have taken place,' says Galdeas. 'You have the Left moving towards the centre. You have an ex-radical guerrilla commander, Joachín Villalobos, proclaiming his conversion to social democracy. This disorientates and confuses people, and I'm sure that the most disoriented of all is probably Joachín Villalobos himself.'

The ambiguous ending of the war and the compromises and ideological transformations that it has involved have generated considerable controversy and debate in Salvadoran intellectual circles about the value of the conflict itself. Was the war, as some believe, a heroic effort by the country's progressive political forces, which finally brought democracy to El Salvador? Or was it nothing more than a senseless act of barbarism, whose final results were not worth the 100,000 lives that were lost to achieve them? For some Salvadoran writers, especially those who went into exile, the war is a shameful episode in the country's history, during which El Salvador became synonymous with violence and atrocity. For these writers, exile was in one sense a positive experience, since it removed them from the ideological straitjacket in which the country was enclosed and enabled them to connect into international cultural and intellectual circuits that had been previously inaccessible to them. 'As a writer, you go outside this country and you don't exist,' says Castellanos Moya, 'no one's heard of you. Unlike other countries in Central America, everything about El Salvador is associated with war and political violence. Even Roque Dalton, our most famous poet, is more well known inter-nationally because of the way he died than for what he wrote.'

Among those writers who stayed in the country and participated in the war, however, the perspective on the decade of armed conflict is very different. Miguel Hueso Mixto is one of those who stayed. Journalist, documentary film-maker and one of the country's foremost poets, Hueso Mixto is an interesting man. Before the war, he wrote poetry and literary journalism, while making a living working for an automobile magazine. As the political crisis of the 1970s deepened, he became increasingly involved with the burgeoning revolutionary movement, until he went to the mountains of Chalatenango to work on a clandestine propaganda radio station for the popular liberation forces in 1982. Like many others, Hueso Mixto believed the war would be over within a year. Instead, he remained in the mountains until 1992, as propagandist, reporter and combatant, in charge of a column of forty guerrillas. Today, he works in an office in San Salvador and continues to write poetry, as well as articles on politics, literature and aesthetics. 'There are some writers who regard the war as an act of stupidity', he says, 'and it's true that there were errors and stupidities committed on both sides, but the war was also a courageous and noble attempt to transform society. I saw peasants who had lost everything and still continued to fight. I couldn't go running into exile in Mexico or Canada. I stayed to fight with them, and I think it was the right thing to do.'

Throughout the war, Hueso Mixto continued to write poetry, in circumstances far removed from the literary circles he had once frequented in San Salvador. 'I used to write every morning between 6.00 and 8.30 before starting work on the radio. I would say that poetry was one of the things that gave me strength to endure the war. I always carried my poems with me, and the thought that one day I would be able to publish them again in one, two or even ten years was one of the things that really kept me going.'

At the same time, Hueso Mixto admits that it was not always easy for an urban intellectual to reconcile his literary vocation with his life as a guerrilla. 'My public consisted of other guerrillas, often peasants who couldn't read or write, whom I used to read my poems to at literary workshops. This forced me to simplify my style a lot, which was good in some ways, but at the same time I always thought that my real public was in San Salvador.' In 1986, Hueso Mixto experienced a personal crisis and asked the leadership for a six-month leave of absence to go and write poetry full-time. The request was, not surprisingly, turned down and he remained in the mountains until the end of the war.

The essentially optimistic and even lyrical vision of the war expressed by war poets like Hueso Mixto is a long way from the moral dilemmas explored in Galdeas' *The Lecture*, or the sleazy stories in Horacio Castellanos Moya's latest collection, which portray with graphic unpleasantness the moral corruption of urban Salvadoran society during the war. Yet all these conflicting attitudes, of celebration, confusion and disgust, reflect different aspects of the conflict and the experience of the generation which lived through it, both inside and outside the country. And, in spite of the differences between these three writers, all three of them share the same belief in the need for artistic independence in the postwar era. Even Miguel Hueso Mixto, once a member of the central committee of the FPL, has abandoned political activity since the end of the war in order to become a full-time writer. 'I think that this country needs to be changed', he explains, 'and that poetry and literature have a contribution to make, but we won't do it by reproducing party lines or ideological visions of the world. If literature can stir people's imaginations and prevent the loss of historical memory, then it will already have achieved a lot.'

For Geovanni Galdeas, even the notion of literature making a 'contribution' is suspect in itself. 'Before, we wrote to educate the people; we used to write from the point of view of having already understood the world scientifically, through marxism. Now I'm writing from the point of view of someone who doesn't understand the world at all. I'm not trying to teach anything to anybody.'

*   *   *

So far, there is no sign of any postwar literary 'movement' emerging among Salvadoran writers and it is difficult to imagine one emerging in the future. In a country where only a tiny percentage of the population read books and magazines, the 'diversity of voices and positions' among a handful of urban-based intellectuals may seem irrelevant. Yet, as the country tries to assimilate the cataclysm that has taken place and rebuild for the future, the individual testimonies and visions of its artists will play a part in that assimilation process. Nor are their conclusions valuable only to Salvadorans. The terrible struggle that took place in El Salvador was perhaps the last major battle in the ideological schism that has marked the history of this century. For most of the world, the 'end of history' took place in 1989; in El Salvador it began three years later. After more than a decade of revolution and social upheaval, the tiny republic that Gabriella Mistral called *el pulgarcito*, the 'little thumb' of Central America, has taken its place in the new world order, with its horizons distinctly lowered. 'I think that the way the war ended, without winners or losers, demonstrates that this country is as confused and uncertain as any other,' says Geovanni Galdeas. 'No one believes anymore in poetic visions of a glorious future and the need to struggle for the revolution. The notion of linear progress towards a better world has disappeared. We are not going forward. We are not headed for paradise or the Garden of Eden.'

Barcelona   MATTHEW CARR
December 1993

Book reviews

Taking sides: the juvenile fiction of Rhodri Jones

'Look Sambo', the policeman said, 'I'll give you some advice. If you want to live in this country you've got to behave yourself. Not that anyone wants you here. Because they don't. If we could get rid of you tomorrow just like that then we would. And we're going to be watching you all the time. You put one step out of line, and we're going to get you. Understand?'

This is an extract from Rhodri Jones's powerful juvenile novel, *Delroy is Here*, first published by Adlib in 1983. It tells the story of a black teenager, Delroy Ellis, of his clashes with racist authority and of his conflict with his father. Delroy is cast in the role of everyman and his experiences are meant to show the reader what life is like for young black males in Britain today. The book is, as we shall see, tough and uncompromising. It was to be the first of a series of novels that Jones was to write in the course of the 1980s, a body of work that has a unique place in contemporary juvenile fiction.

There are today an encouraging number of radical novelists writing subversive, oppositional, children's and juvenile fiction. Robert Leeson, Malcolm Rose, Jan Needle, Gwen Grant, James Watson and Robert Swindells are among the most notable. Mention should also be made of the late Robert Westall, without doubt one of the most accomplished post-war writers of juvenile fiction, whose anti-war novel, *Gulf*, is one of the most powerful and moving fictional indictments of the Gulf war written for any audience. Of particular interest, however, is the anti-racist fiction of Rhodri Jones, fiction that explores the black experience in Britain with humour, passion, realism and commitment.

Jones, a former teacher and headteacher, is perhaps best known for his contribution to the English curriculum in schools, as the compiler of a number of standard school poetry collections exploring everyday life and multicultural experience. His *One World Poets* collection, which includes poetry by Claude McKay, William Plomer, Gabriel Okara, Edward Kamau Brathwaite, Zulfikar Ghose and others, is a good example. It is his own fiction that really deserves attention, however. Since the appearance of *Delroy is Here* in 1983, he has published another six novels: *Hillsden Riots* (1985), *Getting It Wrong* (1986), *The Private World of Leroy Brown* (1987), *Different Friends* (1987), *So Far To Go* (1987) and *Slaves and Captains* (1988), and one short story collection, *Them and Us*, which was first published in 1991.* This body of work falls into two sections: the first three novels are stories of resistance, of anger, of fighting back. This is very much a reflection of the scale of the resistance to the Thatcher government: the 1981 riots, the 1984-85 miners' strike and the Broadwater Farm insurrection. These novels celebrate fighting back and sustain the belief that the system can be beaten. The other novels and the short story collection are all tales of retreat. They are not about confrontation and struggle, but are instead concerned with survival. The one exception is *Slaves and Captains*, which will be discussed separately.

Fighting back

Delroy is Here follows the adventures of its hero at home, at school and on the streets. Although a bright, likeable lad, Delroy is continually at odds with his authoritarian and unsympathetic father, is always in trouble at school and falls foul of the police. Jones's portrayal of school life is determinedly unsentimental: he makes clear that Delroy is no angel, conniving with his friend Bradman's bullying and extortion of smaller kids. The scene where he and Bradman are caught smoking in the toilets, where their guilt is absolutely beyond any shadow of doubt but they still both resolutely deny the offence, is absolutely authentic.

Jones describes a social studies lesson where Delroy is bored rigid. He

> had finished clipping his nails. He tried to get back to his book, but he couldn't concentrate on it. Why were they always on about immigration anyway? They were always making laws and regulations about it. Once someone had asked Mr Andrews how many black immigrants there were in Britain, and the teacher had said about three per cent. Delroy had been amazed that the number was so small. 'What are they so scared for then?' he had asked. Because everyone did seem to be scared. Everyone seemed to be terrified... People sometimes called him an immigrant, but he had been born here.

---

* All published by Adlib, except *So Far to Go*, published by Canongate.

Delroy's attitude towards school is mixed: the lessons are a waste of time, but he really enjoys basketball and is even in the school team. This causes trouble at home which climaxes with his father throwing him out of the house.

While the scenes of home and school are convincing, the most powerful section of the book concerns Delroy's relations with the police. Jones does not pull his punches: 'A state of war existed. The police were the enemy. All the boys could give examples of how they or their friends had been victims of police harassment.' On one occasion, when Delroy and his friends are 'moved on', a policeman warns him: 'Don't try and play clever tricks with me, Nigger boy, because you won't succeed.' Later, after he has been thrown out by his father, he is stopped by the police. He has done nothing, but this, of course, does not save him from intimidation and humiliation:

> Delroy was suddenly spun round and thrust face forwards against the wall. His nose hit the brickwork, and the sharp pain made tears spring to his eyes. His arms were spread wide above his head. The palms of his hands were ground into the grittiness of the surface. His legs were jerked violently apart so that he almost fell... Delroy felt tears of humiliation and shame join those of pain. He was so helpless. They could do anything to him. He clenched his teeth, determined that the tears would not flow.

This racist harassment is not confined to the streets. Delroy is the victim of a racist teacher at school, Mr Frobisher. The book ends with Frobisher finally pushing him too far, with Delroy hitting him, an assault that the book clearly endorses.

Delroy is Here was followed in 1985 by the *Hillsden Riots*. This is a fictional account of the 1981 riots, in particular of events in Brixton in London. It follows the experiences of two brothers: Colin, a studious sixth former with a white girlfriend, determined to get to university, and Wayne, his younger brother, who is always in trouble at school and prefers the streets to homework. Wayne is bitterly hostile to the police, and when a riot breaks out in Hillsden, he gets swept up in it.

Police intervention in a stabbing incident precipitates an attack on the officers involved by a growing crowd. A police car is overturned. The confrontation quickly escalates into a full-scale riot as hatred of the police brings hundreds of people, black and white, on to the streets. To Wayne, it 'seemed as though the world he knew had been totally transformed. They had let the police harass them and humiliate them, but now the worm had turned... They were going to fight back.'

Jones provides a graphic account of the nights of rioting, an account that sides unreservedly with those fighting against the police:

> It had been a real battle all right with the enraged mob facing the

line of police. Each time, the pattern had been the same. The crowd slowly moved forward. One or two of the braver spirits – or more incensed – advanced a step or two in front, yelling defiance and hurling a missile. The crowd pushed forward to back them up and join them. Then the police charged, striking out viciously with their batons, seizing a straggler here and there to pull behind their lines, driving the crowd back. They could see their comrades, now prisoners, being set upon, booted and clubbed and dragged along the road. The crowd's fury erupted once more, and threats and anger and bricks were thrown at the police. They would advance again, and the police would counter-charge.

Sometimes, one of the policemen got too eager and found himself stranded in the hostile mob, away from the protection of his colleagues. Then the crowd was on him like wild animals, his helmet was knocked off, his shield kicked away, his baton wrested from him, and all weapons were used against him – fists, nails, knees, feet. Wayne had never seen faces so distorted with hatred and the desire for revenge. In the few blows the crowd were able to land before the policeman, bloody and staggering, was rescued, were packed the bitterness and resentment of years.

Wayne takes part in an organised attack on a local National Front pub, the Queen's Arms. The police are driven off, the pub is stormed and then set on fire. When the fire brigade arrive, the police turn the hoses on the crowd and charge. As he tries to escape, Wayne is clubbed to the ground.

Alongside the riot scenes, there is Colin's education in the reality of black life in inner-city Britain. He is sent to try and find his younger brother and instead runs into Herald, a former school acquaintance, who is now unemployed and living in a squat. Herald has become a black revolutionary. He tells Colin, 'you don' know you born...

You ever been pick up by the police on a charge o' obstruction when all you do is standin' in the street? You ever been 'rested by the police and made to strip to you pants while they stares at you an' laughs an' makes jokes? ... You ever get t'row in a bull van like a sack o' potatoes an' 'ave you 'air pull an' you 'ead bang 'gainst the wall? You ever get take to court on the say-so o' a bullman who 'ate you guts an' tell more lies than a weigh machine? When that 'appens to you, then maybe – jus' maybe – you might know the 'aff o' it.

The conforming, respectable Colin reminds Herald of the Invisible Man, not the H.G. Wells story, but the one by a black man, Ralph Ellison. ''E show 'ow the only way white society gonna accept a black man is if 'e so goody-goody, they don' even notice 'im or 'is colour. 'E become invisible. That what you is, boy. You've become invisible.'

Colin is being trained 'to be one o' they meek little lap dogs.' They will show him off as a success story: ''Ere we 'as a black man what made it... You ain't gonna call us prejudice when we 'llows that, is you.' Colin decides to take sides.

Hillsden Riots is a quite remarkable celebratory account of the riots that broke out across much of inner-city Britain in 1981. While both Colin and Wayne have reservations and doubts about violence, nevertheless the story, the description, carries the reader along with those who are fighting it out with the police. The riots are a spontaneous revolt against oppression, an uprising by people who have had enough and are at last fighting back. There is no mistaking where Jones's sympathies lie. The result is one of the more remarkable works of juvenile fiction, a novel without precedent, that has been quite astonishingly ignored by both the Left and, perhaps more surprisingly, by the Right.

Getting It Wrong is a grim account of how two black teenagers, Clive and Donovan, respond to being arrested, beaten up and charged with a crime they didn't commit. It is, Jones informs us, based on 'actual events'. The two boys are on holiday, bored, and so, with her permission, they borrow Donovan's Auntie Elsie's organ for a jam session. While taking it home, they are stopped by the police, beaten up and arrested for having stolen the instrument. Once again, Jones tells an unsentimental tale about convincing characters: Clive is indeed a petty criminal, a chancer. On this occasion, however, the two boys are fitted up and fed into a justice system where the odds are overwhelmingly stacked against them. The novel explores the effect that the affair has on their lives.

At their trial, the police tell a pack of lies and Auntie Elsie's evidence in their defence is ignored. They are both convicted and given a year's conditional discharge. Donovan is outraged: 'They call themselves the law and justice. That was a laugh. They'd broken more laws and done more wrong in a few hours than he had in his whole life.' Even the boys' liberal teacher, Mr Abbott, in court as a character witness, sees 'the last vestiges of his faith in the police ... slip away'.

This tale of injustice is told with real anger. Already, though, the belief in the efficacy of fighting back is beginning to weaken. While Clive is determined to get his own back, Donovan, the more sympathetic character, just wants to forget the whole incident and put it behind him.

Surviving

Jones published three novels in 1987 and they all involve a retreat from the politics of his earlier work. The first, *The Private World of Leroy Brown*, is written for younger readers, the 10 to 14 age group, than his other novels. It is very much a traditional school story of escapades, narrow escapes and tables turned, all recounted with comic effect – but with a black protagonist. Here, the teachers are benign (even Mr Garfield mellows in the afternoons after he has had a lunchtime drink) and the world is friendly. This is a different universe from the *Hillsden Riots* and *Getting It Wrong*.

Second is *Different Friends*, another outstanding work of juvenile fiction. The story is told in the first person by a Greek boy, Chris, who recounts his realisation of, and coming to terms with, the fact that one of his friends, Azhar, a boy from Singapore, is gay. Chris is the concerned, troubled observer who tells the reader of Azhar's struggle to survive, a struggle that sees him eventually driven to attempt suicide. The final outcome is hopeful, however, with Azhar living happily with his lover, Jeff, and Chris in the process of getting off with Katina. This is still a world of mass unemployment and racism, but they are in the background, barely visible, while attention is focused on Azhar and on the difficulties of being a gay teenager. Jones once again creates convincing characters and the result is a marvellously sensitive novel. Nevertheless, the politics of *Different Friends* are very much concerned with surviving in the world as it is, of making space and finding a haven, rather than of fighting back and trying to change it.

The third of the 1987 novels is *So Far To Go*, a particularly depressing book. It is a story of defeat made all the more debilitating by the way in which the central character resolves to make the best of the consequences. A white Scottish family move from Glasgow to London, where the father has found work as a corporation dustman. Here they hope to make a fresh start. Young Ian, the protagonist, has trouble settling in, but eventually strikes up a friendship with a black kid, Vincent. Then disaster strikes. The council privatises its refuse disposal and Ian's dad once more faces the prospect of life on the dole. There are scenes of resistance, of fighting back. The council meeting is picketed:

> There must have been about two hundred of them packing the steps of the town hall and spilling out onto the forecourt. Most of them had placards which they held up high and brandished about. Ian read, SAY NO TO CUTS, NO PRIVATISATION, SAVE OUR JOBS, SERVICE NOT PROFIT.
>
> Whenever anyone approached who might have been a councillor, the people surged forward towards him and the chanting began. A passage was formed so that he could get through the crowd to the entrance, but he was urged on all sides to oppose the cuts and save jobs. Some councillors stopped and listened and argued or gave their support. Others pushed through stony-faced as though they weren't even aware there were other people there.

The campaign fails and the family's plight is compounded by his mother losing her cleaning job as well, and Ian's elder brother being jailed for thieving. Vincent's dad has already been on the dole for six months and now decides to take his family, including Vincent, back to Jamaica. Ian is to lose his best friend.

He finds consolation, however. He has befriended old Bill, the man who looks after the gardens attached to a block of private luxury flats. This is a 'secret garden' that no one visits, certainly not the local yuppies. Here, Ian finds a haven, a sanctuary from a world of troubles. Old Bill promises that he will see to it that Ian takes over as gardener when he retires. Jones seems quite unaware of how grim this prospect actually is. Seduced by the literary conceit of the secret garden, he fails to recognise the scale of the retreat he is endorsing. Becoming gardener for a block of private flats is not surviving to fight another day, but surrendering. Similarly, with Vincent's return to Jamaica. The novel's bleak and pessimistic resolution is very much a reflection of its times, with its author not seeming to realise just how little hope he is offering.

Jones's short story collection, *Them and Us*, published in 1991, is still concerned with survival but is decidedly more lively. It consists of eight stories that explore the experiences of very different kids, both black and white. They range from Richard, who makes false alarm calls to the fire brigade, to Marilyn, excluded from school for calling the headteacher 'a silly cow', to Beverley, who is determined to get to university despite a racist headteacher, to Shane, an instantly recognisable racist and proto-fascist. All these stories are well-observed, superbly crafted and a pleasure to read. While still concerned with individual survival, the protagonists are beginning to fight back, trying to change things.

This brings us to *Slaves and Captains*, a rewrite of Herman Melville's *Benito Cereno*. Here, the liberal, kind-hearted Captain Amasa Delano comes across a slave ship in difficulties on the high seas. He goes to its assistance, finding a disturbing, unsettling situation on board, although he cannot quite put his finger on what is wrong. The ship has lost many of its crew and has only been saved with the help of the slaves, but something is not right. Even though he is a liberal, humane man, Delano's racism prevents him from solving the mystery of the *San Dominick*. He just cannot conceive of slaves being capable of acting independently: all the evidence that is right in front of him, showing that the slaves are in fact in control of the ship and the crew are their prisoners, is interpreted differently. This is a disturbing mystery story with a powerful message, a well-written, fictional exploration of the limitations of liberalism.

Conclusion

Rhodri Jones has provided us with a number of remarkable fictional accounts of Britain in the 1980s. The anger of the early novels was very much a literary response to the resistance that the Thatcher government encountered in its early years. The different concerns of the later novels, concerns that focus more on survival in difficult times, reflect Thatcher's apparent triumph. After the defeat of the miners, the Tories seemed unassailable and Jones wrote stories of Azhar finding a haven with his lover, Jeff, and of Ian taking shelter in his secret garden. Now, as Tory Britain collapses around us in a mess of corruption, incompetence, sleaze, bigotry, injustice and reaction, the time has come for something different, something new.

Bath College of Higher Education   JOHN NEWSINGER

Waterfront workers of New Orleans: race, class and politics, 1863-1923

By ERIC ARNESEN (New York, Oxford University Press, 1991). 353pp.

That world trade has cycled over the backs of stevedores and other dock workers, these many centuries, seems little more than a truism. Still, not much attention has been lent their particular role in local, national or global economies, and precious little is generally known of the labouring class cultures of prominent port cities. Few groups in labour history are as central to the operation of the world economy and fewer still are detailed studies of their political and social behaviour.

   The past fifteen years have witnessed a somewhat corrective trend in this direction. Recent detailed studies of the political organisation and social life of dock workers in London, Liverpool, Bristol and Marseilles; Havana, New Orleans, Mobile and Mombasa, point up the density of accumulated sociological issues and materials that charac-terise the world's historic ports. Still, the 'port as crucible' of cultural metamorphosis and the dock worker as agent of that process remain, as yet, somewhat virginal perspectives.

   Today's preoccupations, whether popular or professional, are far from the world of waterfront labour. In the United States, the image of dock workers, like that of manual and blue-collar labourers generally, is constructed mainly via media fantasy. Key stereotypes probably include Paul Robeson's moving (1936) interpretation of 'Ole Man River' in Jerome Kern's *Showboat* (a naive (re)presentation packed with charged southern imagery), and Marlon Brando's striking performance in *On the Waterfront* (1954). As the recent studies clearly indicate, dock work is historically dirty, dangerous and oft times degrading. Dock workers have rarely heeded Marx's exhortation to unite globally, though most have at one time or other formed or joined major unions. The political savvy of dock workers has tended to run ahead of the working class generally, due to the cosmopolitan contacts their labouring venue affords and the occasional stranglehold they can exert on regional and national commerce.

The demographic complexity of ports, together with the nature of their skills, produces this special segment of the working class – one that has played a major role in conveying information, as well as musical, sartorial, linguistic and even aesthetic models from one area of the world to another, contributing to mass culture its own distinctive perceptions of worker politics and popular styles. The Argentine tango and early New Orleans jazz/dance forms are conspicuous examples of the kinds of symbolic clusters contrived by dock workers who moonlighted as entertainers. Port workers and their allies, mariners, have always synthesised heterogeneous varieties of aesthetics and performance with motifs from their respective regional hinterlands.

Ports tend to be urban complexes with a difference. Imagine, for example, Britain (or Ireland, for that matter) without Liverpool, France without Marseilles, Cuba without Havana, the Deep South without New Orleans, or Florida *sans* Miami. Such image-laden urbs have come to signify entire nations and cultures, but they also evoke the respective working classes who derive their sustenance from loading, warehousing and shipping the globe's commodities. Ports and their dock personnel have synthesised and transmitted those intangible, unconscious communications (vibes) that unify humanity. Ports have been perennial incubators of popular culture – of the symbolic and material data which, once appropriated by national bourgeoisies, invariably emerge as hegemonic in fashion and taste.

The shrill vociferations and easy camaraderie of today's New Orleans riverfront workers (a remnant of their pre-second world war numbers) are echoed throughout the commercial entrepôts of the pan-Caribbean – of which the 'Crescent City' is merely the northernmost point. If ever a population's experience lent itself readily to an exploration of the dynamic between racial and class determinants of political behaviour, New Orleans dock workers are such a group. Eric Arnesen's account of the black and white cotton screwmen and other crafts who worked the New Orleans docks from the Civil War era to the first world war, provides a special view of this topic, drawn essentially from the local press. The author selected the theme because 'no adequate, scholarly study of African-American social, political and economic life in late nineteenth-century New Orleans currently exists' – a fair generalisation, perhaps, though Daniel Rosenberg's (1988) study succinctly covers much of this same ground.[1]

Mr Arnesen presents a skilful exploration of the difficult terrain over which native waterfront labour, desperate immigrant groups, ex-slaves and commercial elites all vied for a share of the port's unprecedented commercial exchanges – a considerable prize since New

Orleans' trade surpassed even New York's in the early nineteenth century. In 1834, New Orleans 'ran ahead of its mighty Northern rival in the value of its exports [mainly cotton] and maintained that particular leadership for nearly a decade'.[2] With a population of over 300,000 in 1900, it was the country's second port and the home of many former slaves. Between 1880 and 1910, the city's black population exceeded 80,000, about 27 per cent of the total and one of the largest concentrations of black people in the US. But black political activity, carefully nurtured during Reconstruction, had been seriously circumscribed by white 'redeemer' coercion, and the number of registered black voters in Louisiana declined from 127,000 in 1890 to fewer than 1,000 by 1924![3]

Race relations in the 1880s were continuous with the antebellum pattern. That is, the previous centuries weighed more heavily upon the society than did any nuance introduced during Reconstruction. Despite the pattern of disfranchisement, remarkable progress occurred in the formation of interracial organising in the cane fields and on the docks, especially through the 1880s. The author directs his inquiry to this phenomenon, tracing the struggle among waterfront workers, from Reconstruction through the 1920s, for cross-craft and cross-racial control of jobs and wages, against the city's international commercial elite.

The modern reader will be aghast at the frustrating conditions that made the collaboration of crafts and races so difficult and at the unseemly role of the state in assuring the interests of those elites. We see how the various castes and skills jockeyed to assure their respective craft's security, occasionally acceding to the logic of joining with wider groups to protect wages and other amenities, again retreating into private agreements with management. In short, the vicissitudes specific to dock work are drawn with clarity and exemplary effort.

At the top of the labour structure were the cotton screwmen. Working in crews of five, attaching cotton bales to the ship's hold, they received $20.00 per day before the Civil War and $31.00 by the 1880s – the best-paid workers in the city or in the entire South. At the bottom were the mainly black roustabouts, whose lives were often dreary. There were over 10,000 men working the docks at the turn of the century, though they were not the only organised labour force. There were over 7,000 steam rail employees and some 600 black tobacco employees in 1900. Foreign seamen visited the city routinely and many were trade unionists, with their respective struggles and solidarity which doubtless influenced the southern ports.

Organising presented a major challenge to labour leaders. For example, 'While most white unions came to oppose the admission of employers to the [labour] council, the sketchy evidence suggests that some black workers, at least initially, welcomed their presence.' The workers' careful manoeuvring to sidestep the shipping companies' crafty manipulation of divisive racial differences draws our admiration.

By the 1880s, an unprecedented level of rural organisation was achieved via the docks, extending the Knights of Labor to the country-side, where they mobilised 1,000 white and 9,000 black sugar cane workers. Hell rained down across Lafourche Parish in 1887 as the state's militia fought to end the strike, which concluded in the so-called 'Thibodeaux massacre'. On 23 November, fifty black workers lay dead and scores of others injured.[4] In 1892, a general strike was called, as over 20,000 workers from forty-two unions walked out of New Orleans' docks during November – the peak commercial season – paralysing the city. The ruling class reacted as a horse with a bee sting: allied with the governor and state militia, they fought back, defeating the workers (who none the less made a good show of their force).

The high point of labour power was reached in the last decades of the century as an umbrella structure, the Cotton Men's Executive Council, consisting of various unions, saw one association join while another dropped. The author patiently discloses how organisations like the Cotton Men's Executive Council succeeded (from the strike of 1881 to 1886) in protecting the jobs and wages of its members and its multi-racial membership, though it 'failed to sustain the inter-trade and inter-racial collaboration that lay at its core'. Between 1886 and 1887, waterfront unions divided along lines of trade and, to a lesser extent, race. 'What began as a triumph of solidarity over craft ended with the triumph of craft over solidarity.' After 1894, 'the remnants of the council finally collapsed amidst racial recriminations', but 'interracial union organising resumed a decade later, and overall, the interracial cooperation was unprecedented in America'.

To summarise, before 1880, racial and organisational divisions kept black and white dock workers fragmented and weak. Then, from 1880 to 1894 and 1901 to 1923, black and white joined in a series of alliances, allowing them to 'expand their collective power over the conditions of labour', all during a period of deteriorating race relations in other sectors of urban life. This is, in part, explained by the context of local politics, the indulgence of the Irish-inspired democratic party machine, with its patronising of the large (frequently Irish) working-class elec-torate. For four decades, the interracial federation of waterfront workers exerted control over the labour process. By the early 1920s, they fell victim to the 'open shop' drive that devastated labour nationwide, as the Depression brought a glutted labour market, with all that implied.

The author is concerned with more than a narrow labour history. The otherwise straightforward treatment is interwoven with a dis-tracting secondary theme: a quest for the 'black community'. To identify and sort out the political behaviour of a large urban mass is a sufficiently daunting task, but to properly characterise a 'black community' in this context is surely illusory. Predictably, the author encounters a series of social contradictions that obstruct his well-intended objective.

Works of history really speak to contemporary issues, so it would be hard to imagine this excellent book (a sorely-needed monograph) without the past decade of union insurgency in Poland and the precipitous decline in the political power of organised American labour. Mr Arnesen's investigation of the nexus of race and labour in a teeming port city is competent, cogent, at times compelling, but falls flat in the trope of current race mythos. He laments that 'flexible racial codes, the absence of overtly discriminatory legislation, and racial proximity in riverfront neighbourhoods produced little in the way of substantive integration'. If black and white men occasionally frequented the same brothels, barrel houses, bistros and gambling dens in certain water-front neighbourhoods, 'there is little evidence that blacks and whites led anything but segregated associational lives ... New Orleans whites and blacks, like those in other Southern urban centers, inhabited separate worlds.' One wonders just what the author expected to encounter. Though the formal topic is waterfront labour organising, the subtext is closer to Uncle Tom's Cabin.

Aside from these imponderable assertions and the author's insistence that we share an unstated totalising vision, the reader is curious that the author has not gathered that New Orleans was the most racially interactive and tolerant city in the South. Rather, he is dissatisfied at having found something less than a multiracial utopia. Since he is so desirous of having his *dramatis personae* share the same bed and board, he might have perused the federal census schedules of 1880 and those following to discover that such arrangements were legion. One senses that New Orleans is being put retroactively to the current 'multiculturalism' test. Oddly enough, this very locale, from 1699 to the American Civil War, saw the most intensive process of 'creolisation' to occur in North America.[5] Because this exceptional regional experience occurred under a series of European colonial regimes and antebellum slavery, it is apparently thereby invalidated and unmentionable.

Though the text considers the role of black waterfront workers in union organising and radical protest, the context veils a broad rhetorical query concerning the nature of black urban society. How is it organised and how does it work? How does it interlock with other components of urban social structure and to what effect? The line of inquiry is diverted *de rigueur* into a mystic liberal paradigm that conflates research with morbid moralism. The social pathologies of non-white groups (note that the 1890 census classified many creoles, American Indian descendants and Asians indiscriminately as 'colored') are not considered. Inter-ethnic dynamics are reduced to a sort of static white racism. The 'official' strategies of exclusion or containment of non-whites are not closely examined, for example the process by which authentic black leadership was (is) suppressed and a corps of acceptable self-styled spokesmen substituted.

All too often, liberal academia seeks to integrate black America by empathetic posturing. Local, collective self-sufficiency and mass economic reorganisation are eschewed. And the sojourn of the black working class since the popular effervescences of the 1920-30s and 1960s? The disposition of the black bourgeoisie vis-à-vis the increasing current immiseration of black America? How is 10 per cent of the US population (25,000,000 people, a body larger than many modern countries) diverted from the careful organisation of its own capital and industrial infrastructure, from pooling and investing its energies and funds, from coordinating and serving its own neighbourhoods?

To a greater extent than elsewhere in the nineteenth-century US, New Orleans' African-descent population was a complex composite of varied sources, culturally penetrated by an equally diverse, bi- and multilingual white propertied class. Though the diversity of the local white population is easily conceded and frequently celebrated (its geographical origins include Canada, France, Spain, Haiti, Cuba, the US, Central America, Sicily, Germany, Yugoslavia and Ireland), the non-white majority is popularly regarded as monolithic and generic – just 'the niggers'. This group constitutes the core of Mr Arnesen's study, but even this segment of the 'nonwhite' population was and remains considerably more heterogeneous than officially perceived or publicly acknowledged.

The author's weightiest source consists of commercial and newspaper reports and surviving minutes of union meetings. Like the rest of America in the post-bellum decades, New Orleans supported a wide range of papers, including French, German, Spanish and other language editions – an immensely rich source of sociological data and local colour. But withal, one senses an imbalance derived from the author's seeming innocence of social theory, which leaves the study rather flat and, *le mot juste*, one-dimensional. We are wont to inquire more of the details of maritime capitalism; of a sharper characterisation of the shipping firms and other institutions that sought to reduce workers to ciphers. How did workers fit into the overall network of plans, projections and profits? What political framework had evolved in the former French and Spanish colonial capital to facilitate or to discourage labour organising, in contrast to the northern/eastern experience? There emerges no clear picture of the national context, since there seems no theory of the state or sense of Louisiana's role in the national hegemony. A foreign country acquired by the US in the early nineteenth century, the region's sub-national, neo-colonial, hybrid character is productive of the most extraordinary mutations, including benign interracial contact within both slavery and post-emancipation racism.

Lastly, an account of labour's struggle seems denuded without some faint excursion into working-class culture. Despite occasional references to brass band performances at labour rallies and parades, the intensely musical orientation of the native working-class population (if not the Sicilian, Irish and other immigrant groups) is not touched upon. Since they were the single largest segment of organised labourers, the dock workers' unique subculture broadly affects the city's working-class aesthetic and general artistic character. (Jelly Roll Morton – Ferdinand LeMenthe Mouton – had been a dock worker, a cotton screwman.) As popular arts often tell us a great deal about their creators and consumers, a brief sketch of the leisure-time activities of the dockmen could amplify our picture of the working class. Few American areas persisted so long in the indulgence of such *déclassé* diversions as public transvestism, cock and bull fights, bare-knuckle boxing and occasional duelling. As it is, no palpable social descriptions emerge in *Waterfront Workers*.

The period with which the author is concerned (1880-1920) is arguably the most confusing and contradictory in southern (and in particular, local) history. Despite the inherent difficulty of the research and the bizarre effects of certain naive assumptions, the author has crafted an excellent monograph in the contemporary mode, and has wisely confined his focus in a style plain and unpretentious; he has heeded both mentors and the signs of the times. Yet, unlike his predecessors, LaSalle, Iberville, l'Abbé Prevost, Audubon, Chateaubriand, Lafcadio Hearn, he may have turned a deaf ear to the sirens of the Mississippi.

Reading this attractive tome induces an admittedly furtive nostalgia for Buster's, for many decades the second home of French Quarter marginals, where, back in the early 1960s, a plate of ribs cost only 50¢. The taste was exquisite, but when one tired of picking over those bones, it was questionable whether the morsel finally ingested was worth the struggle. Extracting the real account from its ideological packaging may similarly affect readers of this important work.

University of New Orleans   THOMAS FIEHRER

References

1 Daniel Rosenberg, *New Orleans Dock Workers: race, labor and unionism, 1892-1923* (Albany, NY, 1988).
2 Roland Osterwies, *Romanticism and Nationalism in the Old South* (Baton Rouge, 1967), pp.158, 155-71.
3 Henry Dethloff and Robert Jones, 'Race relations in Louisiana, 1877-1898', *Louisiana History*, IX, no.4 (Autumn, 1968), pp.301-23.

4 Thomas Becnel, *Labor, Church and the Sugar Establishment: Louisiana, 1887-1976* (Baton Rouge, 1980), pp.16-18; Grady McWhiney, 'Louisiana socialists in the early 20th century: rustic radicalism', *Journal of Southern History*, XX, no.3 (August 1954), pp.315-36.
5 Joseph Tregle, 'Creoles and Americans', in A. Hirsh and J. Logsdon (eds), *Creole New Orleans* (Baton Rouge, 1992), pp.131-85.

Rethinking Camelot: JFK, the Vietnam war and US political culture

By NOAM CHOMSKY (London, Verso, 1993). 172pp., £9.95.

The 1963 assassination of John F. Kennedy has probably inspired more conspiracy theories than any other political killing this century. Culprits as disparate as the KGB and CIA, Fidel Castro and ultra-reactionary Cuban emigrés, and a host of others have at various times been accused of bringing an abrupt end to Camelot-on-the-Potomac and depriving America of an Arthurian leader who alone could have prevented the social and political turmoil of the ensuing years.

More recently, thanks largely to Oliver Stone's movie, *JFK*, and the associated flood of publicity, the theory that Kennedy was killed by a high-level conspiracy because he intended to extricate the United States from Vietnam has gained ascendancy, particularly among the American Left. Key forces in government, the military and the intelligence community, we are told, could not countenance the prospect of withdrawal and therefore acted to replace Kennedy with an allegedly more hawkish Johnson, perhaps with the latter's knowledge. And, having successfully covered up their monumental crime, it is held entirely plausible that this 'secret team' has been running the affairs of state ever since.

In addressing these issues, Noam Chomsky returns to the debate on America's involvement in Indochina; a debate which, at the height of the war a quarter of a century ago, he helped initiate and influenced more than any other dissident intellectual. And, where others have since publicly recanted, he has expanded his critique of American foreign policy and will only admit to a deep sense of shame for not opposing the war earlier.

Rethinking Camelot does not address the Kennedy assassination as such. Rather, it asks whether the conclusion that Kennedy intended to withdraw from Vietnam can be deduced from the extraordinarily detailed historical record. And secondly, it asks whether there was, indeed, an abrupt change in US policy towards Vietnam in the year after Johnson took office. As Chomsky makes clear, evidence is needed not just to demonstrate that Kennedy was committed to a withdrawal from Vietnam – even his most hawkish advisers intended to leave if the National Liberation Front ('Viet Cong') was defeated – but specifically to establish that he, at least, contemplated withdrawal without military victory. Only then would the assassination theory have a basis in fact.

The painstakingly-researched findings are as unambiguous as historical scholarship permits. Simply put, there is not a hint in the voluminous documentation that Kennedy ever recognised Vietnam as an unwinnable war or considered cutting his losses. Instead, it consistently 'portrays JFK only as less willing than his top advisers to commit himself to withdrawal – and surely not without a victory'. Similarly, the record reveals no abrupt change, in fact no change at all, in America's Vietnam policy during the first year of Johnson's tenure.

What Chomsky does find, or rather reaffirm, is of equal interest, given current efforts to rewrite the history of this era. This is that Kennedy, during 1961-62, dramatically intensified the American role, inherited from Eisenhower, from one of supervising state terror by the Diem regime to one of direct aggression, subsequently bequeathed to Johnson. Thus, when the latter launched a major escalation of the war in early 1965, it was not a change of policy but rather a change of tactics necessitated by the erosion of the American position on the ground. As Chomsky persuasively argues, the doctrinal framework, policy goals and team of presidential advisers remained unchanged throughout this period, and he demonstrates that the US recognised from the outset that it could never compete politically with the NLF and saw the massive and indiscriminate use of violence as its only option. For these reasons, 'the belief that JFK might have responded differently ... is an act of faith, based on nothing but the belief that the President had some spiritual quality absent in everyone around him, leaving no detectable trace.'

Rethinking Camelot does not deal with allegations that Kennedy was assassinated over a change of heart towards Cuba in the same detail. However, it points out that US-sponsored terrorism against Cuba 'broke entirely new grounds' after the failed Bay of Pigs invasion, and that it was Johnson who, in 1964, terminated what he described as 'a damned Murder, Inc. in the Caribbean'.

As with so many of Chomsky's writings, a good number of pages are devoted to exposing the fraudulence of intellectuals. In this case, the victims are the Knights of Camelot themselves, who, prior to the 1968 Tet Offensive, had no inkling of Kennedy's alleged intent to withdraw without victory but, in the aftermath of the NLF's demonstration that this was their only choice, emphatically recalled that discussion at the Round Table had resulted in precisely this conclusion. Other liberal 'doves', who consistently praised American intentions and objectives and found fault only with the methods of execution and results, are, in turn, juxtaposed with the more sober assessments of the military establishment. Certain, at least, is that not even the most extreme dove ever ventured an opinion similar to that offered by Marine Commandant General David Shoup in 1966:

I believe that if we had and would keep our dirty, bloody, dollar-crooked fingers out of the business of these nations so full of depressed, exploited people, they will arrive at a solution of their own. That they design and want. That they fight and work for. [Not one] crammed down their throats by Americans.

St Antony's College, Oxford   MOUIN RABBANI

For Palestine

Edited by JAY MURPHY (New York and London, Writers and Readers Publishing, 1993). 252pp., $14.95/£10.99.

For Palestine charts the course and the cause of the struggle for Palestinian liberation. Covering the ten years from the Israeli invasion of Lebanon to the US/Allied forces' destruction of Iraq in the 1991 Gulf war, this collection of articles, poetry and interviews is not a history book or a turgid academic tome, but an example of what so many writings on the Arab world could and should be: a tool for liberation.

Through the testaments of the fighters in the poverty-ridden slums of the refugee camps, to interviews with Palestinians and contributions from journalists and anti-imperialist writers, we hear of the fight for Palestinian independence, freedom and self-determination.

From Mary Howell's 'Ansar III: the camp of the slow death', where Palestinians are detained without trial and often tortured in the 'banana position' (hands and feet are tied together behind the prisoner's back), to letters from West Bank residents to relatives in the US describing life under curfew during the Gulf war, *For Palestine* provides us with a moving collection of pieces on Palestinian political culture, enabling us to understand the everyday living of stateless people.

Jean Genet, visiting the scene of the Shatila massacre, tells in 'Four hours in Shatila' how he came 'to understand the obscenity of love and the obscenity of death'. Others consider the impact of the *intifada*, five years after it erupted in Jabalya refugee camp in the Gaza Strip, and the state of the Palestinian women's movement. Noam Chomsky and Hanan Ashrawi are among those interviewed.

To demonstrate to us the coinciding interests of Israel and the US, one chapter describes how criticism of Israel is stifled through the censorship of 'pro-Palestinian' documentaries and films. The Anti-Defamation League and the American-Israel Public Affairs Committee are among those creating the definitions of censorship buzzwords ('unbalanced!', 'partisan!'). Definitions which viewed a simple film of an ordinary Gazan refugee family's life under occupation as PLO propaganda.

The only criticism of this book is of the editors' hope that the United Nations can somehow be an independent force for progressive change, regardless of the US or the foreign policy interests of other member nations. Nevertheless, as the negotiations over the Palestinian bantustan continue, *For Palestine* reminds us that there are still many, many issues to be dealt with; that the scars of occupation and of torture will not heal easily; that, despite the public belief that the 'Palestinian problem' is being resolved by politicians, the struggle for Palestine is only begun.

London   SUJATA AURORA

One Dark Body

By CHARLOTTE WATSON SHERMAN (London, The Women's Press, 1993). 209pp., £6.99.

The title of Charlotte Watson Sherman's novel is borrowed from a citation by W.E. DuBois on the two-fold nature of the African-American experience: 'Two souls; two thoughts; two unreconciled strivings; two warring ideals in one dark body, whose dogged strength alone keeps it from being torn asunder.' It is both the twoness that threatens destruction and the courageous struggle for history and identity that *One Dark Body* recounts.

It is the story of Raisin who, even before her birth, must know pain: the pain of entering a world which doesn't want her, of entering into a history which has already betrayed her. Grandmother doesn't want her because Raisin's presence recalls her own betrayed love. Mother doesn't want her because, at 15, pregnant, she is already widowed when her boy-lover, defeated and world-weary, commits suicide. The other children don't want Raisin because her skin is wrinkled, like a raisin – hence her name. It is also the story of Sin-Sin who, fatherless, feels rejected and lost. He must learn how to live with his special gift: an eye in one hand that can peer into the past and the present.

But with this pain and this loss, there is also the healing, when both Raisin and Sin-Sin learn to live with their histories and to take pride in their special traits. Nola, Raisin's mother, comes back to explain about her father and to prevent Raisin from falling into another whirlpool of self-destruction. In piecing together Raisin's fragmented identity, Nola learns about herself: how she, like her mother, betrayed her daughter for the love of a man. The novel shuffles back and forth between the perspective of the three generations of women, illustrating mother-daughter conflict and its ongoing resolution.

Healing also comes from Blue, the wanga-man, a shamanic figure who lives in the forest and who initiates Sin-Sin into manhood and teaches him the age-old ways of his people, thereby reinstating an unbreakable cycle of history. Blue becomes the father that Sin-Sin never had, a father who transmits knowledge and know-how in a world where biological fathers have disappeared mysteriously and violently at the birth of their offspring.

By substituting fabricated but unbroken genealogies of words and knowledge for biological but destroyed genealogies, Sherman is commenting on the history of the African-American family and the ravages that slavery and racism wrought on it. But she is also describing the struggle for history and the search for identity in an attempt to keep this history and this identity part of living experience. This struggle comes through not only in the narrative itself but also in the poetry of the language and in the mythic structures of the imagery. In the magical descriptions of the rites of initiation and of the forest, colour predominates: black, orange, red, green, blue and white. Colours of Africa. Colours of skin. Colours woven into the fabric of the novel and the consciousness of its characters in an attempt to reclaim history and to teach self-pride.

At times, however, these descriptions seem a little too obvious in their imagery and a little too concerned with mythic poetry, as if Sherman has sacrificed the specifics of the African-American experience for elementary and universal structures of the mind. Moreover, at times, the rites of passage read more like poetic anthropology and less like a novel, more like a series of isolated descriptions and less like a tightly constructed form. But then, *One Dark Body* is a first novel and with it, Sherman is promising to perfect her craft and to master the form.

University of Geneva   SABA BAHAR

Ecofeminism

By MARIA MIES and VANDANA SHIVA (London, Zed Books, 1993). 328pp., £12.95.

The title of this first co-production by Maria Mies and Vandana Shiva, *Ecofeminism*, is bold, but promises too much. Although many a pearl is tucked away in its 300 or so pages, it amounts, basically, to a compilation of thought-provoking essays by the two major feminist proponents of a radical and populist critique on development, capitalism and ecological destruction.

With their pathbreaking books *Patriarchy and accumulation on a world scale* (Mies, 1986) and *Staying alive* (Shiva, 1988), Maria Mies and Vandana Shiva gave ecofeminist thought a cutting edge and linked it to radical critiques of development. But they have not done all the work alone. During the last twenty years, ecofeminism has united critiques of women's and nature's oppression. The title, *Ecofeminism*, led me to expect a continuation of this fruitful strand of thought, but, in fact, only five pages of explicit consideration are given to eco-feminism as a whole. Moreover, scattered references to other writers do not redress an overall failure to acknowledge the work of others. Many an author has, through differentiated and thoughtful analyses, contributed to ecofeminist thought and the lack of consideration given to them effectively belittles their work and boosts *Ecofeminism*'s achievement. Furthermore, the book contains many repetitions and material (sometimes acknowledged, sometimes not) from a host of former publications by Mies and Shiva.

Ecofeminism consists of twenty essays, grouped in six parts, with a conclusion. Part one introduces the authors' feminist research method, based on a critique of western scientific epistemology. Then, part two, 'Subsistence v. development', outlines a general critique of the global political economy. Parts three and four, on the 'Search for roots' and biotechnologies, turn to more specific topics. Some of the points made in part three, which concentrates on the links between the globalisation and the uprooting of life on the one hand, and nationalism and romanticism on the other, were inspiring but not satisfying. What seems to be implicit is the idea of 'good' vs. 'bad' nationalism – which, in my view, does not sufficiently question the concept of 'nation' as fundamentally exclusive, as 'we and them' and as socially constructed. Therefore, it cannot explain how, historically, nationalism turns openly violent.

The chapters on biotechnology contribute to an interesting debate on body politics, in particular in their critique of the limits of liberal feminism. This, through its approach to the body as 'private property', actually allows the state – the protector of property – to control the female body more closely, even in the midst of feminist endeavours to liberate women. The theme of freedom, liberation, self-determination is continued well in part five, which illuminates the different views on freedom held by liberal feminists and liberal economy brokers, in contrast to the concept of freedom held by the Chipko, an Indian forest protection movement with a strongly female basis.

Part six and the conclusion then take up various topics (quite a lot of repetition here) to elaborate on a truly liberating strategy, through a mixture of global networking and grass-roots initiatives around 'small-is-beautiful' ideas. While I agree with these ideas and always admire the authors' ability to link global analysis with local real-world examples, I would have preferred more openness about what the application of these strategies implies, i.e., the hope of eventually transcending modernity by a dialectical continuation of it. For example, you cannot network globally or publish books without being a modern actor in a modern world of high technology, money resources, etc., but this is not brought out.

What is fascinating, however, is the ability of both authors to lay out how and why the dynamics of the global capitalist system are inseparable from sexist, racist and eco-exploitative structures of patriarchy, Third World development and domination over nature. Their analysis is pursued with a holistic critique of modernity. An intrinsically hierarchical process, modernity has a history of expropriation hidden behind the neutralist mask of alleged gains for humanity as a whole: progress, economic growth, ever-rising consumption, scientific exploration. But this progress is the growth of cash, knowledge, power for men, for urban upper classes, for white people, for humans as opposed to nature. It is based on plunder and robbery, now just as much as 500 years ago. Thus, growth and power for the few means actual deterioration for ecosystems, poverty and growing ignorance for many Third World people, dependency and violence for women. Arising from this, Shiva and Mies argue convincingly that any struggle for liberation will be incomplete if it is built on the continuing subordination of anybody else, or of nature.

It is, indeed, refreshing to hear from two radical critics of global sexism, racism and ecological destruction at a time when so many writers seem ready to compromise, consciously or not, in the face of the 'New World Order' and the so-called 'greening' of capitalism.

University of Sussex   STEFANIE LAY

Free to Hate: the rise of the Right in post-communist Eastern Europe

By PAUL HOCKENOS (London, Routledge, 1993). 332pp., £17.95.

As the Berlin Wall came down in 1989, the conservative philosopher and much-feted literary figure, Francis Fukuyama, declared the 'end of history'. Paul Hockenos, in *Free to Hate: the rise of the Right in post-communist Eastern Europe*, corrects this anti-Communist fairy-tale. 'In 1989 history did not perish – it was reborn', he writes.

This is not to say, however, that nationalism had been 'unborn' in the Communist state. As BBC World Service journalist Misha Glenny had previously argued, 'Nationalism was refracted through the prism of Stalinism' and the product was a grotesque hybrid of both ideologies. Hockenos, Central and Eastern European correspondent for *In These Times*, develops this argument further. Romania, for instance, turned its back on Stalinist internationalism. But Ceausescu's 'national communism' excluded the Romany and the Hungarian minority in Transylvania. Many Hungarians were forcibly moved from Transylvania to 'agro-industrial living complexes', while Transylvanian villages with a strong Hungarian identity were bulldozed or resettled.

The point is, however, that the post-war Communist states were born out of, and drew legitimacy from, the defeat of fascism. And if, at Communism's birth, fascism was declared dead and buried, then it followed that no de-nazification process was necessary to educate the people out of fascist, racist and eugenicist ideas. Hence, with the collapse of Communism and the fracturing of the state along ethnic fault-lines set in an earlier history, the cataclysmic effects of Communism's failure to develop an alternative anti-fascist political culture (as opposed to an official anti-fascist state ideology imposed from above) are only now being felt.

Too many journalists, when embarking on a study of the far Right, are sucked into a neo-nazi world of conspiracy and subterfuge which tends to blur any wider political vision. The strength of Hockenos' study – of Germany, Hungary, Romania, Poland, the Czech Republic and Slovakia – is the clarity of its focus. At one moment, Hockenos is interviewing key nationalist figures like Istvan Csurka, the leader of the anti-Semitic Hungarian Justice and Life Party, or Czech demagogue and Republican party leader Miroslav Sládek; at another, he is providing a worm's-eye view of the skinhead world. But he never loses sight of the wider object of his study, the rise of the ethnic state.

Free to Hate is written in a journalistic style, combining first-hand reporting, original documentation and political analysis and, as such, its sweep is broad but never superficial. True, Hockenos tantalises you with themes he does not have the space to develop, but then it is up to the reader to travel further. Two themes particularly interested me. More needs to be written in English about the influential German 'Neue Rechte', the stated goal of which is to 'bring the German Right out of the shadow of Auschwitz'. The most original of Hockenos' chapters is 'Poland: Christ of nations'. Polish anti-Semitism, Hockenos shows, should be seen in relation to Catholic fundamentalism and the close alliance between state and church. The rise of Christian fundamentalism throughout eastern Europe (and indeed Europe as a whole) is an issue that Hockenos has placed firmly on the political agenda. It is one that urgently merits further attention.

But if these are the book's major strengths, it does possess two rather glaring weaknesses. Although Hockenos readily admits that anti-foreigner violence and hatred of the Romany are more virulent in the countries that he has studied than anti-Semitism (not least because nazi concentration camps wiped out Jewish populations), his major focus is on anti-Semitism. There is nothing wrong with this in itself, but it does mean that other important themes, like the anti-Arabism that characterises Hungarian racism and the state deportation programmes of former guestworkers across eastern Europe, are not touched upon in the detail that they deserve.

More importantly, when it comes to comparing eastern Europe to western Europe, the clarity of Hockenos' political analysis suddenly falters and fails. Hockenos argues that the situation in eastern Europe would be improved if western-style democracy and the values of the free market were embraced. At the same time, he concludes that the enforced economic devastation brought about by the IMF and western austerity programmes are strengthening the populism of eastern Europe's demagogues. There is something of a contradiction here. Political pluralism and the development of civil society is indeed needed if eastern Europe is to break out of a cycle of authoritarianism, nationalism and fascism. But is the free market really the economic system to bring about political pluralism?

Hockenos' failure to see the dynamic relationship between east and west today is all the more disappointing in that, throughout the book, he makes a vital distinction between eastern European 'ethnic states' and the 'civic nation states' of western Europe. Eastern European nationalists, Hockenos argues, elevate the ethnic or national community to a position above state or citizenship. And the 'primacy of blood establishes a racial hierarchy of people'.

The irony is that western Europe is moving away from the 'civic nation state' to a more exclusive concept of citizenship and the primacy of blood is being written into western Europe's citizenship laws. Maybe western Europe's more civilised democratic sensibilities are offended by the Csurkas and the Sládeks of this world (we do not use the language of the past, we are not so crude, we are post-fascist), but we are in the process of developing our own racial hierarchies in immigration laws that exclude not only people from the Third World, but our fellow Europeans. For racism today, as Sivanandan has recently argued in the introduction to *Inside Racist Europe*, 'is about prosperity, and prosperity is white, western, European... The asylum-seeker ... is invariably non-white, or, if white, non-prosperous, un-settled, an itinerant from Eastern Europe.'

Hockenos has begun to open up a little understood, yet vital, subject. It is one that will profoundly affect the political future of western Europe also.

Institute of Race Relations   LIZ FEKETE

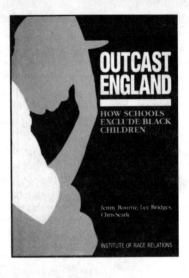